TRADITIONAL VALUES FOR TODAY'S NEW WOMAN

Previously published as
The Flip Side of Liberation.

HOPE MacDONALD

Zondervan Publishing House
Grand Rapids, Michigan

A Division of HarperCollins*Publishers*

Traditional Values for Today's New Woman
formerly *The Flip Side of Liberation*
A Call to Traditional Values
Copyright © 1990, 1992 by Hope MacDonald
All rights reserved

Requests for information should be addressed to:
Zondervan Publishing House
Grand Rapids, Michigan 49530

Library of Congress Cataloging-in-Publication Data

MacDonald, Hope.
    [Flip side of liberation]
    Traditional values for today's new woman / Hope
MacDonald.
      p. cm.
    Previously published as 'The flip side of liberation.'
    Includes bibliographical references.
    ISBN 0-310-54831-4
    1. United States—Moral conditions. 2. Liberty. 3. Liberty—
Religious aspects—Christianity. I. Title.
HN90.M6M33   1992
241'.0973—dc20   91–3364
                                            CIP

Printed in the United States of America

92 93 94 95 96 / CH / 6 5 4 3 2

To my children and their families,
my joy and constant blessing

Tom and Wendy
Breelyn

Dan and Kathleen
Megan and Jenny

Debbie and Marc
Scott, Shane, and Skye

Other books by the same author

Discovering How to Pray
Discovering the Joy of Obedience
When Angels Appear

TABLE OF CONTENTS

Acknowledgments

I want to thank my beloved husband, Harry MacDonald, for his constant encouragement and faithful prayers during the writing of this book.

I would also like to thank the congregation of the John Knox Presbyterian Church in Seattle for their prayers. Each Sunday I was reminded of their love, prayers, and excitement over this book.

I would never attempt to write a book without a small group of committed, praying friends. These friends prayed for me faithfully each writing day until the book was completed. Their prayers are much a part of this book. My special thanks to

Nada Bohnette	Helen Leonard
Patti Bylsma	Marilyn Mead
Anne Cheirs	Beverly Miller
Marlys Hardie	Jane Short
Marty Heaps	Patty Taylor
Pat Kelly	

PART
ONE

OUR
IMPRISONED
RELATIONSHIPS

''Eternal vigilance
is the price of liberty.''

THOMAS JEFFERSON

ONE

The Wall
of Shame

Freedom by itself is never free.

O̲N AUGUST 13, 1961, a tragic event took place in the name of liberation. The East Berlin government erected a concrete wall that suddenly separated people from one another. Brothers and sisters, children and parents, friends and relatives found themselves imprisoned behind a crude barricade of arrogant hopelessness.

My husband and I and our three children first saw the wall on a clear fall day in 1963. The brilliant blue sky was filled with sunlit clouds. Yet a feeling of apprehension swept over us as we left the crowded streets of beautiful West Berlin to climb the steps of the wooden platform that enabled us to look into East Berlin. The first thing we noticed was the absence of people on the other side. Streetcars went by without passengers and we saw no cars in either direction. The scene was much different from the happy people walking about the streets of West Berlin. We found ourselves whispering to each other out of respect for all the pain, heartache, separation, and death the emptiness represented.

On Sunday afternoon we saw both sides of the wall crowded with people who came to wave to each other—a mother blew kisses to her little children, and a husband waved to his wife. One young woman held up her baby, trying to show a new tooth to the grandmother on the other side. Many older people stood at the wall and wept. I saw a little brown sparrow fly over from East Berlin and thought, "Only the birds are free over there."

This was the only wall ever built by a nation to keep its people *in*. In the free world it is known as "The Wall of Shame." Yet it was built in the name of freedom and liberation.

When I review the events that have occurred in the United States during the past twenty years, I wonder if an invisible wall of shame is being built around this nation in the name of liberation. Have we fallen for a counterfeit freedom that is locking us into a prison of hopeless depravity? Are we becoming a people ruled by the ever-changing winds of general consensus in which each person does what is right in his or her own eyes?

In this liberated age have we forgotten that freedom by itself is never free—is never enough? It must always be accompanied by responsibility. No society in history ever survived when its rights became separated from its responsibilities. Has our nation's newly acquired lifestyle enticed us into a perverted sense of freedom so that now we are held fast in a prison of liberation?

For example, look at what has happened to our relationships with one another during the past few years. More marriages are broken by divorce in our country than in any other country worldwide. As a result, children are separated from parents just as the concrete wall separated families in Germany. In the name of liberation the rate of pornography, abortion, homosexuality, drugs, and immorality flagrantly rises and our wall of shame grows higher with each passing year.

We forget that a culture is judged by the way its people are treated, and relationships are judged by the way we treat one another. We ignore the ominous truth that we are in danger of becoming a nation of isolated individuals living in a lonely world of broken relationships. Our liberated society is languishing in a prison of death-producing diseases, broken homes, unwanted pregnancies, aborted babies, and overstressed single parents. It seems that, as a nation, we are sinking in a quagmire of shattered dreams and disillusionment. "Our World is filled with self-absorbed, frightened, hollow people."[1]

We are permitting things to happen that we never imagined would happen. Among these is forgetting how to discern right from wrong. Even the national judicial system, that used to know right and wrong, is no longer sure of what is moral or immoral, what is pornography and what is art, or if it is right to take an innocent baby's life. Chaim Potak asks, "Six thousand years of civilization has brought us to this?"[2]

We have witnessed a disintegration of moral and spiritual values across our land since the first stone in our wall of shame was laid over twenty years ago in the early 1960s. In that decade we experienced an unparallelled deterioration of moral and spiritual values. As a result, our homes and relationships with one another are in constant chaos. In many instances our family life is now nothing more than an aching void. Human nature, freedom, and justice are becoming dangerously out of balance.

As citizens, and as human beings, we can no longer remain silent and indifferent to the destructive forces that have crept into our society and homes in the name of liberation. We have been rocked to sleep in the hammock of apathy long enough. As a united people we have a responsibility to ourselves and to future generations to rise up and dismantle the wall of shame that surrounds our country in the same way East Berlin has done. Let's remember that the goal of East Berlin's recent revolution for freedom was to regain the human dignity stripped away when the first brick was laid in the wall four decades ago. Are we willing to wait forty years before we begin to rebuild this nation on the foundation of justice, truth, and honor? Will our children have to say, as Wolf Biermann, the East German poet said after the wall finally came down, "I must weep for joy that it happened so quickly and simply. And I must weep for wrath that it took so abysmally long."[3]

We have been led astray both as a nation, and as individuals. The false promises of liberation are fast becoming a sad lament. Edmund Burke said, "The only thing necessary for the triumph of evil is for good men to do nothing." We need to read, study, and become aware of what is happening in the world around us, and then get involved in changing what is taking place in our country—reemphasizing the role and importance of our homes and schools. The words of Thomas Jefferson, "Eternal vigilance is the price of liberty" have been forgotten. We have been out of tune with one another and God's principles too long.

This book is a call for renewal. Its purpose is to alert us to how great a role liberation has played in building a wall of shame around this country. We must seriously think about what is taking place and actively concern ourselves with the moral and spiritual values governing our land.

This is also a book of hope—reminding us of the eternal truth that God works in individual lives today. He works within nations to bring his people closer to him. And he can restore the broken relationships that lie scattered all around us.

May God direct your thoughts as you read through the following pages.

As Louis L'Amour once wrote: "Reading without thinking is nothing. For a book is less important for what it says than for what it makes you think."

TWO

Let Freedom Ring!

No society in history ever survived when its rights became separated from its responsibilities.

Most of us love our country and are willing to die for it. Since its beginning the United States has stood for liberty and justice for all, as well as for freedom and human dignity. In addition, it is respected around the world for its compassion. But the one feature that sets the United States apart from all other countries is that it was built upon the foundation of the existence of God and operates under the moral and spiritual laws of the Bible. Reading through the U.S. Constitution and the Declaration of Independence makes a person feel blessed, inspired, and proud to be an American. Today the country's creed still remains, "One nation under God, with liberty and justice for all." This truth is repeated every time we recite our pledge of allegiance.

Our country is great because of the wise and courageous actions of our Founding Fathers. I was reminded of this on my first visit to Washington D.C. It was cherry blossom time, and the entire city lay covered under a lacy canopy of pink flowers. I visited one historical landmark after another and jotted down some of the writings inscribed on our national monuments. Each time I reread them I am filled with pride.

(1) Above the head of the Chief Justice of our Supreme Court are the Ten Commandments showing the great American eagle protecting them. (It is now against the law for any public school to display them).

(2) On top of the Washington Monument, for all of the world to see, are the words, "Praise be to God!"

(3) Throughout the halls of the Library of Congress are many quotations from the Bible.

(4) Beneath that magnificent memorial to Abraham Lincoln are numerous references to God, the Bible, and to our Lord Jesus Christ.

(5) At the Jefferson Memorial are the powerful words: "God who gave us life gave us liberty. Can the liberties of a nation be secure when we have removed a conviction that liberties are a gift of God? Indeed I tremble for my country when I reflect that God is just, that His justice cannot sleep forever."

And on our money we read the words, "In God We Trust"—an overwhelming proclamation for a nation to make. When my husband and I visited India a few years ago, we were invited to dinner at the home of an Indian family. Upon our arrival the entire family—all of the children, aunts, uncles, and grandparents—greeted us with open curiosity. We were the first Americans that they had ever had in their home.

After dinner we sat around the table visiting. At one point my husband, Harry, gave some American coins to the children. After carefully looking at the change, one of the older boys asked what was printed on the coins. When Harry replied, "In God we trust," the entire room became quiet. Then everyone wanted to see the money. They reverently held the coins and asked, "Do you mean ALL of your money says, 'In God we trust?' " They thought the United States must be a special nation to have such a statement printed on its money.

Yes, we do live in a great country. No other nation in history has been founded upon such solid principles of truth and freedom, with God the Creator as its cornerstone. However, we are beginning to see this country's foundation crack. God has been removed from much of American culture. With the weakening of our foundation, nothing remains sure or secure. Secular humanism, which says, "Man is the measure of all things," seems to reign supreme.

I live in Seattle, Washington, which is called the Emerald City because of the surrounding natural beauty of the evergreen trees. The sparkling blue waters of the Puget Sound and many nearby lakes reflect snow-covered mountains. But downtown, old picturesque buildings are being torn down and replaced with modern offices made of steel and glass. I asked one of the city planners why so many of the old landmarks had to be demolished. He said, "The foundations are crumbling, and it's too late to save them."

Today, America's foundation is also crumbling, and it must be saved before it is too late. Restoration can begin by changing our attitudes toward our nation, education, family life, and society.

THE NATION

The foundation of Western civilization began to show tiny cracks back in the mid-sixteenth century when René Descartes made his revolutionary statement, "I think, therefore, I am." Will Durant calls this "The most famous sentence in philosophy." From this starting point, the doors of the Enlightenment swung wide open to science, math, philosophy, physics, music, and art. The Enlightenment enabled us to have many of today's conveniences. But along with it, man was elevated to the position of God and became the final authority for defining the physical universe and setting the parameters for moral and spiritual values. God was put in a box and man decided that our country's religious foundation was no longer adequate.

The Enlightenment insisted that to explain a thing we need only specify its physical and chemical causes; any thought of meaning or purpose in ordinary reality must be excluded. God is no longer needed; we can get power over the world by dealing directly and solely with the natural laws which operate in it.[1]

In 1859, Charles Darwin wrote the thesis, "On the Origin of Species by Means of Natural Selection." The theory of evolution sprang from his ideas and continues to influence both thinking and teaching.

Karl Marx and Friedrich Engels published *Das Kapital* a few years later, in 1867. This atheistic philosophy is based on the assumption that man is the measure of all things and therefore the master of his own destiny and the creator of his own fate.

The writings of Friedrich Nietzsche followed in 1882. He promoted the concept of the superrace and was one of the loudest proponents of the theory that God is dead— therefore we need to create a superrace whereby man can adequately control his destiny through social structure.[2]

EDUCATION

Another crack in our nation's foundation is in the area of education. When Harvard University was established, the requirements for enrollment included that each student consider that "the main end of his life and studies is to know God and Jesus Christ which is eternal life."[3]

The common goal of Yale, William and Mary, Princeton, Dartmouth, and Columbia was "to educate young people in the spirit of Jesus and the Bible."[4]

Noah Webster, one of the great educators in Western civilization, declared: "To give children a good education in manners, arts and science, is important; to give them a religious education is indispensable."[5]

These goals, and so many others, were the foundation upon which our educational system was built. Compare the above standards with recent events in our country.

"This year, the school board of Los Angeles was sued to prevent any mention of God in the student's graduation speeches. A settlement was announced between the school board and the American Civil Liberties Union that in graduation ceremonies of that huge school system, 'No prayers or any mention of God will be allowed.' "[6]

Every form of prayer was removed from our nation's schools in 1962. Through our nations courts, the ACLU eliminated the right for a child to even pause for a moment of silent prayer. During these changes most of us sat idly by and watched this godless progression of events. Children in our nation's schools can no longer sing Christmas carols, and manger scenes are forbidden. Public prayer and benedictions are also prohibited in community meetings.

Billy Graham believes the day is coming when "Prayers cannot be said in Congress, chaplains will be taken from the armed forces, and the President will not place his hand on the Bible when he takes the oath of office."[7]

When the foundations of the nation and education begin to crumble, the foundation of the home follows. And with the home goes the culture, our society, and eventually our lives.

THE FAMILY

It is a proven fact that a nation is only as strong as its families. Destroying the family destroys the nation. If our nation is to survive, we must rebuild our families. We have listened too long to those who degrade family life.

> Marriage has existed for the benefit of men and has been a legally sanctioned method of control over women. . . . We must work to destroy it. The end of the institution of marriage is a necessary condition for the liberation of women. Therefore, it is important for us to encourage women to leave their husbands and not to live individually with men.[8]

This kind of thinking threatens the core of our nation.

We must start rebuilding family life if freedom is to continue to ring out across our land. Marriage must once again become a lifetime commitment, and children must be taught, by both parents, the moral and spiritual values this country was founded upon.

OUR SOCIETY

In the United States' search for total liberation it opted for a self-destructive lifestyle that is affecting the unborn to the elderly. With our beliefs stripped away, we find ourselves aimlessly drifting on the sea of life without a life raft to cling to or a compass to guide us. "Nobody really believes in anything anymore, and everyone spends his life in frenzied work and frenzied play so as not to face the fact, not to look into the abyss."[9] We end up echoing Kris Kristofferson's haunting words, "Freedom's just another word for nothing left to lose."[10]

However, a new awakening is beginning. We don't like what we see when we look at what the past twenty years has produced. People are reevaluating the results of freedom without responsibility and feel it is time to establish new priorities. A new appreciation for this country is taking root, and we are once again becoming aware that this nation is abundantly blessed with freedom, untold natural resources, health, and wealth. We, the people, are not about to let all these blessings be snuffed out like a candle in a cold draft.

But most important, we are learning that there is no such thing as absolute freedom—we know we can no longer choose to do anything we want with absolutely no consequences. "America has no-fault automobile accidents, no-fault divorces, and it is moving with the aid of modern philosophy toward no-fault choices."[11]

We *are* responsible for the choices we make. They make a difference in our lives, and in the lives of our children, for generations to come. We are coming to grips with the truth that every freedom the Constitution established comes with an equal share of responsibility. "Without a context of limitation, freedom has become dangerous and meaningless."[12] The only workable equation is freedom plus responsibility equals justice for all.

Let Freedom Ring!

Americans love a challenge and we have a tremendous challenge today! If this great nation crumbles, there will never be another one like it. We are called, by future generations, to restore and rebuild the cracks in our country's foundation—making sure that the true greatness of freedom continues to ring out and the stars and stripes fly forever!

Thought Questions

1. Share one or two of your underlined thoughts.

2. How does the building of the Berlin Wall correlate with our current culture?

3. Why is freedom by itself never enough?

4. List five things that make you proud to be an American. (If you have visited Washington D.C., share your personal impressions.)

5. What cracks do you see forming in our nation's foundation?

6. Do you see a new awakening beginning to take place in our country? In what ways?

7. Why is it important to be aware of events taking place in the name of liberation?

THREE

God's Design
for Marriage

*Marriage is the sharing of history together . . .
his story and your story.*

> I do promise and covenant
>   Before God and these witnesses
> To be thy loving and faithful wife/husband
>   In plenty and in want,
> In joy and in sorrow,
>   In sickness and in health,
> As long as we both shall live.
>
> Whom God hath joined together,
>   Let no one put asunder.

WITH THESE or similar words, a marriage is born.

Marriage is one of God's great gifts to His creation—a gift to be reverently cared for and tenderly nurtured. God alone is the Creator of marriage. When He performed that first wedding joining Adam and Eve in the Garden of Eden, He stamped His seal of eternal blessing upon this holy sacrament. (A sacrament is an inward gift of grace demonstrated through an external act.) Marriage is sacred in God's sight. On our wedding day, when we stand before the pastor or priest, the blessing of God comes upon our marriage. The guests are witnesses to the solemn vows we make before God.

The Bible says God joins man and woman together. This is why it is so important that no one comes between us, or "puts asunder" this holy sacrament. In Hebrew, the word for marriage means consecrated. This means we are set apart, by God, for one another. There is no other relationship more hallowed or blessed in all the world. We have lost sight of these critical principles in our "liberated" society of serial marriages. We have forgotten that when God created us male and female, He created us to have a personal relationship to Him and with one another. He created us to *need* each other. "The Lord God said, 'it is not good that man should be alone. . . .' " With these words, the sacrament of holy matrimony was established and our need for one another was met.

> A person is the most single, most limitless entity in creation, and if there is anything that is even more unlimited and unrestrained in its possibilities than a person, then it is two people together.[1]

What glorious potential we have when living together as one under God's hand of blessing! We have a lifetime to learn about this chosen loved one. Throughout the years we grow to understand more about the necessity of accepting and encouraging one another. As a couple, we discover the pleasure of laughing together, the importance of being able to cry together, and the value of praying together. We learn how to respect and honor one another. As we grow together, we gain insight into our partner's inner being and begin to experience the joy of cherishing one another. All of this may take a lifetime to learn, but since the beginning of time God ordained that our lives be forever enriched through the gift of marriage.

WE BECOME ONE

My husband and I came to a standstill while working on a puzzle one evening. We could not find the particular piece we needed. Suddenly, Harry picked up a small piece we had both looked at many times. He turned it around and dropped it into place. "Oh!" we both shouted, "that's it!" with a happy feeling of satisfaction. Something similar happens when we meet that certain person with whom we long to share the rest of our life. There is a joyful certainty of, "Oh! This is it!" It is a sense of total completeness, like the fitting together of two matching pieces of a puzzle. This is what Adam meant when he said about Eve, "[she] is now bone of my bones and flesh of my flesh"(Gen. 2:23). Elizabeth Goudge refers to it as our "other hand." "Everyone needs someone in the world who is like his other hand."

When two people join in holy matrimony, all of their personal potentials are enhanced. They remain two separate individuals, yet they are bonded together in love—they become one. Even though they are totally different and unique, God says they become a part of one another. "A marriage is not a joining of two worlds, but an abandoning of two worlds in order that one new one might be formed."[2]

The Bible refers to marriage as becoming one flesh. That is a revolutionary concept. "Therefore, a man leaves his father and his mother and cleaves to his wife, and they become one flesh" (Gen. 2:24 RSV). This is a mystery we may never fully understand. One aspect of becoming one flesh is that our values and dreams are directed toward the same goal as we travel together down the same road of life. We know that no two people are alike, just as no two snowflakes are alike. We look different, have different personalities, different likes and dislikes, and different abilities. Yet the Bible tells us we become one when we come together as husband and wife. That is God's design for married life.

> God used the rib of Adam to underscore man and woman's interdependence, "bone of my bones and flesh of my flesh" as Adam expressed it. The two were interwoven, interdependent, interlaced; no fierce rivalry, no hierarchical one-upmanship, no independent autonomy. What a beautiful picture.[3]

Becoming one flesh does not happen instantly. It may take a lifetime to complete.

> God intends for a husband to love his wife and a wife her husband as extensions of themselves. . . . We rarely see this in marriages. It is far more common to see mutual tolerators and coping cohabitors,—and moving toward the less humane—competitors, adversaries, enemies. But every now and then we do see a couple who seem to have become one flesh.[4]

Robert Roberts refers to being one flesh as a "calling" for all Christian couples. And what a high calling it is!

> The Lord God made woman out of part of man's side and closed up the place with flesh, but in marriage He reopens this empty, aching place in man and begins the process of putting woman back again, if not literally IN the side, then certainly AT it.[5]

Matthew Henry said, "God took woman, not from Adam's head to be above him, nor his feet to be below him, but from his side that she might stand next to him." This was always God's eternal plan for man and woman—that they might stand side by side in every area of life.

I frequently tell my husband that he is my most priceless possession. That may sound negative in today's individualistic society where we don't want to belong to anyone except ourself. But we belong to one another when we are joined together in holy matrimony. "My beloved is mine and I am his" (Song of Sol. 2:16 RSV). We give each other not just our love, not just our body, but our very heart. "One heart is given in exchange for another. . . . It might almost be said that love is the total willingness to be owned."[6]

When we give ourself to another, with no strings attached, love is set free to grow and mature. This is what we referred to in our marriage vows with the words, "To *have* and to *hold* from this day forth until death us do part." That is possessive love in all its glory! We give our love and independence to our loved one. In one sense, biblically speaking, we actually lose our life in marriage, but in the losing, we gain a totally new life together. Deep within we begin to experience the joyous certainty that, "Oh! This is it!" And both our lives are forever altered. We belong together and we are one. Love reaches its highest peak when we no longer fear being possessed by our loved one. Because with that possession comes true liberation—the kind God intended when He ordained, and set apart as holy, the marriage relationship.

> The wedding is merely the beginning of a lifelong process of handing over absolutely everything, and not simply everything that one owns but everything that one is.[7]

This is the essence of becoming one.

TRUST

My husband is very proud of his Scottish heritage, and it was with much pride that he took our family to Scotland. We fell in love with the desolate beauty of that mist-covered land. One night we stayed in a thatched-roof cottage tucked away in the cool green forest of the lake country. After a delicious dinner of haggis stew and scones, we put the children to bed. Then Harry and I went downstairs to sit by the warm fire with an old gentleman-grandfather. As he rocked back and forth in his chair, he said something about trust that I have never forgotten. "I'd much rather go through life trusting people and be hurt occasionally, than to go through life never trusting anyone."

Today, the word *trust* has almost disappeared from our vocabulary and certainly from most of our lives. A wife no longer trusts her husband, and a husband is afraid to trust his wife. Children are unable to trust their parents, and parents rarely trust their children. We don't trust our neighbors, our newspapers, or even our elected officials. And far more tragic, we no longer trust God. The unfortunate result of our inability to trust is that we are gradually becoming dry, brittle people. I think that is the truth behind the old Scottish grandfather's statement.

In this day of total "liberation," we have forgotten that trust is the foundation of a lasting marital relationship. Love only grows when it is trusted. When a marriage is built on the solid ground of trust, our love for one another is constantly renewed—love is set free to grow, mature, and ripen like a luscious tropical fruit. When we no longer trust one another, we miss the shining beauty God intended for marriage. Trust means we are completely safe in each other's love. Such trust is deeply rooted in the vows of fidelity we made on our wedding day.

Trust is choosing, by an act of our will, to be faithful to our partner. As a minister, my husband counsels couples who are about to be married. He urges them to understand the importance of being totally faithful to one another, "till death us do part." He advises them to talk about this critical aspect of married life and to reach a positive decision about it. He feels it is imperative that couples understand *why* fidelity is crucial to the success of marriage.

> The sooner you can make up your mind what you really believe about sexual commitment, the better it will be because in the long run what you do about having an affair will depend more on your beliefs than on your feelings.[8]

The foundation of a good marriage is *always* built upon the trust we have in our partner and the vows we made. We must be convinced of the validity and necessity of both. The vows may be brief and simple, but they are extremely profound. They are often the only vows we will ever make. Perhaps that is why they can be so frightening in today's "liberated" society. We must keep our vow to love and honor one another, even after we discover the cost. Mike Mason says, "The saying of them [marriage vows] requires about thirty seconds. But keeping them is the work of a lifetime."

These may seem like old-fashioned views to the modern, liberated person, but they are the truths which, when lived out in daily practice, will prevent much heartache and unnecessary sorrow within marriage.

CREATIVE LOVE

When Mac, our neighbor across the street, was very ill and near death, my husband would go over in the evening to pray with him and his wife, Irene. Sometimes I would go along. One of the beautiful memories I have of this dear older couple, is seeing them sit together in their living room, in the warm glow of the lamplight. Every night before going to bed they would take turns reading verses out of a well-worn Bible. In those sacred moments together, their living room became a quiet chapel. They had traveled together many years down life's rocky, yet sunny road. They had experienced God's truth revealed in 1 Corinthians 13, that his greatest and longest-lasting gift is love. It was God's creative love that became the spiritual force that enabled their marriage to become what it was intended to be in this lost, fallen, and hurting world. They had learned that the ability to love and be loved came from God and was a treasure to be cherished forever.

Creative love is a joy-filled love that touches every area of life and reaches out to all those whom God has entrusted into our care. It is a liberating kind of love—a song of celebration simply because it comes from our loving Creator who ordained it. However, we must remember that love never "just happens." It is consciously established and preserved throughout our years together. Love must be continually cultivated and cared for like a garden. It takes time and a lot of sacrifice. "Love is not some marvelous thing that you feel but some hard thing that you do."[9]

Love is extremely vulnerable in this fragile world. And vulnerability is often an intimidating aspect to incorporate into a marriage. We don't like being vulnerable because it means looking to God for direction in our daily relationship together. It means admitting we need someone outside of ourself. Saying "I need you" to our partner can be very threatening. We like to believe we need nothing. We want to be in control of our life, and the captain of our ship.

Part of this creative, vulnerable love includes submission, a word that is totally rejected by today's "liberated" culture. I think of submission as loving cooperation in every area of a marriage relationship. Just as we submit ourselves to study God's Word and learn more about Him, so we must submit ourselves in loving cooperation, to study our partners, to learn more about them every day. Submissive love not only makes it possible to give love, but also to receive it. Many people are unable to receive love because the act of receiving means there is a need to be met. We often find it difficult to admit how desperately we need one another, or need to be loved. My daughter's husband gave her a little sign that says,

> I don't love you because I need you; I need you because I love you.

We live in such a "liberated" age that an exclusive monogamous marriage is often looked upon as a serious neurosis. Some feminists call marriage "the profound mistake." Relationships become strictly conditional with this prevalent kind of thinking. For example, "I'll stay with you as long as you make me feel good." As a result, the success of a marriage is often measured by the degree of our own personal fulfillment. Subsequently, we live in a world of superficial relationships and temporary commitments.

"All the old foundations for permanence and fidelity seem to have eroded away."[10] We used to fall in love and get married; now we sleep together, live together, and if things work out right, we draw up a marriage contract. Surely, these kind of marriages are found wanting. Such relationships can easily be severed with a simple handshake or a carefree good-bye.

God's creative marriage offers so much more. It is the sharing of history together . . . his story and your story. This shared history unites us as few things in life can. No marriage contract, or live-in relationship, will ever equal the joy of a shared history that springs from a lifetime commitment to each other.

Creative marriage involves sacrificial commitment and trust by both partners at every level. We are bound by the strong, though gentle chord of love which is capable of coping with the stress of everyday living. Love is the energy that ignites the fuse of life, causing a warm glow that engulfs the entire home. Karl Menninger calls it, "a rare and precious jewel." A creative marriage means you love your partner today, tomorrow, and the next day. You will love each other when hair thins or grays or when wrinkles take over and the "love-handles" grow. Marriage is changing together in a changing world. In marriage, we live in a world full of ups and downs. We do not live on a suspended cloud of happiness. The beauty of becoming one and learning to trust comes by learning to share the ups joyfully, and sticking close together in the downs.

Two priceless treasures in my home remind me of my parent's love. One is a lovely antique mirror rimmed in gold and carved with crystal etchings. My father gave it to my mother on the day I was born. The second is my father's leather Bible. The well-worn pages are patched, yellow with age, and covered with his precise penciled notes. This old Bible traveled with him many years, to missions and jails, street corners and churches, where he told the story of Jesus and His love over and over again. I cherish these gifts, but my parents passed on to me something of even greater value—the gift of their abiding love for one another.

We may give many beautiful gifts to our families throughout the years, but the one supreme gift that lives on long after we are gone is the gift of love that we pass on to our children and to our children's children. Love is a gift without price. First Corinthians says this kind of love outlasts anything and never fails.

As wonderful as this love may be, it is only a tiny echo of God's eternal love for us.

Thought Questions

■ ⊏━━━Ⅱ⊏━━━⊐ ■

CHAPTER THREE

1. Share one or two of your underlined thoughts.

2. How do you think God's design for marriage contrasts with today's culture?

3. What image comes to your mind when you think of marriage?

4. In reading this chapter, what important principles were you reminded of which can enable you to be a better partner?

5. List ten good qualities about your partner. (You can divide them into three categories: physical, mental, and spiritual.) List ten of your good qualities.

6. What does it mean to become "one" with your partner? How does this differ from today's concept of marriage?

7. Why is trust a vital part of a marriage relationship? What can you do to maintain this trust?

8. What area of your marriage do you want to work on in order to keep it alive and creative? How do you plan to do this?

FOUR

The Family

"All we really need is a sound roof over our head, a fire to sit by, and a family of our own to love."

Mark Twain

OUR CHILDREN'S favorite neighborhood while growing up was Borland Road, in Pittsburgh, Pennsylvania. I frequently recall spending long summer evenings sitting on the curb with the neighbors, watching the kids play kick-the-can, as we shared the day's events. Then as the first stars of twilight began their march across the sky, we would watch the lightning bugs flash their tiny lanterns as they darted across the lawn. To this day, the lingering memories of those evenings remain a happy treasure.

One of the reasons Borland Road brings back delightful memories is because it was a neighborhood made up of mothers, fathers, and children bonded together by close family ties. No one was divorced, or "living together," and we had never heard the term, "single parent."

Today the uprooting of the American family is cause for great concern. "The traditional American family in which Mom stayed home with the kids, while Dad worked, seems headed for extinction."[1] The monogamous family is disappearing from our society and being replaced by serial marriages, divorce, and a frantic search for personal wealth.

35

Perhaps the decay of the family is happening because we have forgotten our history. Before there were cities, governments, churches, or schools, in fact, before there was any written language, there was the family—established by God at the beginning of time. And it is one of the few remaining institutions of the human race. We must remind ourselves that no society in history managed to survive after family life deteriorated.

In spite of this reality, many proponents of the Woman's Liberation Movement insist that the entire family structure, as we know it, must be completely abolished. Feminists continue to cry out that the family is outdated and the cause of many of our problems. This kind of continual rhetoric throughout the past twenty years has caused family neighborhoods like Borland Road to disappear. Society is unaware that these neighborhoods have been wounded from within and are dying.

Sheila Cronon, one of the leading feminists says, "Since marriage constitutes slavery for women, it is clear that the Woman's Movement must concentrate on attacking this institution. Freedom for women cannot be won without the abolition of marriage."[2] The philosophy of this movement is destroying the very core of our nation. Note the following frightening statement. "Being a housewife is an illegitimate profession . . . the choice to serve and be protected and plan towards being a family-maker is a choice that shouldn't be. The heart of radical feminism is to change that."[3]

These statements have led us astray. Instead of the movement's promised independence, families are hopelessly entrenched in a prison of "liberation." The ultimate collapse of family life is inevitable unless we meet this problem in the same way we, as a nation, gear up to meet other emergencies that threaten our land. We must be as equally concerned about what is occurring in our world as what is happening to family life.

The devil is out to destroy the family as never before. He is successfully bringing about this destruction with the radical liberation movement sweeping across our land. "We must destroy love . . . love promotes vulnerability, dependence, possessiveness, susceptibility to pain and prevents the full development of woman's human potential by directing all her energies outward in the interest of others."[4] Only as we stand firm and "watch and pray," (as Scripture instructs us) can we withstand the fiery darts that continue to be hurled at the family unit through this movement.

When Nehemiah returned to rebuild the wall in Jerusalem in 445 B.C., he took one look at the overwhelming devastation and cried out, "There is much rubbish, so that we are not able to build a wall!"[5] Isn't the same occurring today? We are inundated with the rubbish of the past twenty years. Until we clear away all the ruin that lies around us we cannot rebuild our family structure. Our inner supports are crumbling and the foundations are giving way. Each of us has a responsibility to do all we can to rebuild our shattered families. We must reestablish stable homes where marriage is a lifetime commitment, and where children are taught the moral and spiritual values of life by both parents.

VALUES ARE LEARNED

A number of years ago our family traveled through Germany on our way to Switzerland, where we were going to study with Dr. Francis Schaeffer of L'ABRI. Our red Volkswagen was crowded with two adults, three children, and several well-packed suitcases. The day had been drenched in happiness as we drove through the fragrant woods of the Black Forest. The picturesque countryside was steeped in peace, and the fragrance of flowers dusted the golden rays of the autumn sun. As twilight approached we found ourselves ready for the small inn described in our guidebook. However, we became hopelessly lost looking for it. After spending an hour in a futile search, my husband leaned out from the car window at a red light and asked the driver of the next car if he could give us directions. When he heard the name of the inn, he motioned for us to follow. He didn't tell us *how* to go, he went *with us* and led us to the door.

One of the unfortunate results of the modern "liberated" family, is that we have lost the way. Not only are we as parents lost, but our children are lost also. There is no one to lead us back to God's plan for family life. Who goes to church and Sunday school today? Here in Seattle, less then 5 percent of the population goes to church. Most working parents are too weary to attend church on their one day home. And the little children are tired too. Often they have been pulled out of their warm beds at half-past five every morning to go to the day-care center. They certainly do not want to go any place again on Sunday. The unhappy consequence is that today's children no longer have the same opportunity many of us had for Christian training. There isn't anyone telling them Bible stories. They do not know who David and Goliath were, and they have never heard about the exciting adventures of Moses. There isn't someone teaching them the Ten Commandments or sharing with them the magnificent words Jesus gave in the Sermon on the Mount. They have never memorized Psalm 23 or other great passages of Scripture to help them through life. Most parents are too worn-out to teach their children spiritual values or give them moral instruction. They are too weary to accept the fact that it is in the home where children see a daily model of what to believe.

Today we have relieved ourselves from all responsibility of spiritual training by saying, "I want my children to be able to make up their own minds when they are old enough. They can choose what they want to believe." The entire problem is laid to rest with that statement. We ignore the nagging truth that no child can make a valid decision in a vacuum. We are going to discover, too late, that we no longer have any beliefs to pass on to our children. "When belief disappears, as it has, the family has, at best, a transitory togetherness."[6] Without a strong foundation of Christian beliefs, our house is built upon shifting sand.

The Family

The removal of the moral and spiritual absolutes from society sets the stage for the eventual decline of the family. The family remains the primary educational force of all learning. Yet today, "The dreariness of the family's spiritual landscape passes belief."[7] How sad this is. Psychologists tell us that the family is the single influence that forms the character and molds the spiritual attitudes of a child.

What attitudes of right and wrong are we passing on to our children in our "liberated" families? Have we forgotten that, "The future of a society may be forecast by how it cares for its young?"[8] To train children well, to give them a strong sense of values, to shape and mold a family unit, takes creativity. It draws upon every resource and skill at our disposal and requires emotional, physical, and spiritual strength.

We often make fun of the old television show *Ozzie and Harriet*, but maybe Ozzie and Harriet weren't so far off in dealing with problems. Many family problems were solved over a piece of chocolate cake and a glass of milk. Maybe we need to see more families eating chocolate cake together today!

TOP PRIORITY

My husband and I recently watched the moving story of Mother Teresa. Throughout the entire movie we both observed the radiant look of peace and joy on her face. Her top priority in life was to care for the destitute and give dignity to the dying. No sacrifice was too great on her part to fulfill this goal. And because of it, her life was filled with a deep inner peace that radiated from every part of her being.

Have we, as parents, placed our families as top priority in our lifestyles? It's true that raising a good family requires a lot of work, discipline, and self-denial. It takes love, compassion, and endless understanding. As parents do we make our children feel important and special? Will we look back and say, "Nothing was too much work or too much trouble."[9] Is that our attitude? Whether home is a tenement apartment or a house in the suburbs, it needs to be a place where loving memories are formed and nourished by the support of the entire family. There isn't a more challenging or rewarding task than making a loving creative home. The importance of family love must never be forgotten, because all of the love we will know in life springs from the love we knew as children. Can we say or will our children be able to say, "Our family was so close it sometimes felt as if we were one person with four parts."[10] The family needs to be top priority in our homes. It will make all the difference.

THE CREATIVE FAMILY

Our son Dan was invited to live in a beautiful home during the three years he attended seminary. It was complete with spacious gardens, swimming pool, and tennis court. Although there was a cook who prepared delicious gourmet meals, the children chose to eat their dinners in their bedrooms watching television. During the years he lived there, he remembers only one meal that the family ate around the dining room table. One Saturday, Dan came home for the weekend and arrived at dinnertime. As we were about to sit down, he paused. His eyes filled with quiet wonder and he said, "Do you know how lucky we are to be sitting down together for dinner?"

The dinner hour is the fastest disappearing hour in the American home. My husband recently asked a group of 127 teenagers how many had eaten dinner with their family that night. Twenty-two raised their hands! Family life has become so fragmented that we no longer have time to share a meal together.

One area where we can begin to rebuild a creative family life is to bring the dinner hour back home. It was not many years ago that families ate evening meals together. Delicious aromas of oatmeal cookies fresh from the oven or a big pot of homemade soup simmering on the back burner, complete with hot apple pie, greeted us when we came home from school. Now we have frozen TV dinners or short-order hamburgers with french fries. Preparing nutritious meals for our families takes time. It takes extra planning and effort to make the dinner hour special, but the effort comes with a lifetime guarantee of happy memories.

Following are seven ways to turn the dinner hour into a happy memory:

1. Eat by candlelight the several months of the year it is dark at dinnertime. We decided to eat by candlelight when our children were young. One Indian summer evening we looked out the dining room window and saw five tousled heads pressed against the screen. My children's friends were watching us eat. As they walked down the front steps we heard one of them say, "And they do that *every* night!" Even though our children are now married, my husband and I still have candlelight dinners.

2. If you have a dining room, move out of the kitchen into the dining room after your last child is out of the high chair. Don't save your dining room for company. You will never have anyone more important in your home for dinner than your husband and children. If you must eat in the kitchen, clear away the clutter and put a lamp on the table. (No ceiling lights!)

3. Have each person share the nicest thing that happened or one thing learned during the day. (Even now, before going to bed, I often find myself asking, "What did you learn today, Hope?") This kind of sharing makes the dinner hour pleasant and teaches everyone to look at the positive side of life during the day. The dinner hour should never be a time for discipline or scolding about neglected chores.

4. Look neat and clean for dinner. Teach your children to do the same. Dinner is *special*.

5. Find creative ways to have dinner. For example, during the summer, set aside every Tuesday night for a picnic in the park. Another night have hamburgers and watermelon in the backyard. And don't forget Sunday brunch, or

a good old-fashioned Sunday dinner complete with roast beef, mashed potatoes and gravy.

6. Close each dinner hour with a reading from the Bible or read one of the good devotional books for children. (Do this at least five nights a week.) Have a short prayer asking for any special requests.

7. Take the phone off the hook during the dinner hour. This is solicitors' favorite time to call. Business associates and friends are also likely to call.

OUR CALLING

When our family was asked to go to Brazil and serve as missionaries, we spent much time in prayer seeking God's leading. In the end, we felt *called* to Brazil. It was this sense of calling that enabled us to get through many of the difficult, heartbreaking experiences during the following years. Whenever we doubted being there, we would remember "the call." We were where we felt God wanted us and that is all that matters in life. The same holds true with our family life. If we see our "high calling" from God as establishing a loving, secure home and a healthy relationship with our partner, it makes all the difference in the world.

Our call is to bring up children in a home where two parents love and care for one another, and where we treat each other with kindness, forgiveness, and love. The significance of this call stems from the eternal truth that God established the family, and he is the one who issues the call. He calls us daily to give, "courageous action and suffering love."[11] If the family is going to survive we must take this call seriously.

There are several practical ways to respond to our high calling. One that must remain a top priority is to make sure we always keep the romance alive and glowing in our marriage relationship. We must take time for giving and making love. If we do not love our partner as much as we would

42

like to, we can ask God to put a greater love in our heart for him or her. He will. During the past forty years with my husband, my daily prayer has been, "Lord, as my love for you grows deeper each day, so may my love for Harry grow." God has honored that prayer.

Along with keeping romance alive, and love growing, comes the equal necessity of having fun together as a family. There are many things to do together to enjoy one another. Visit an art museum. This can be a fascinating adventure and a great learning experience. How many children in our liberated society go to art museums with their parents? Save a little money each month so the whole family can attend the symphony or a play once a year. Occasionally go to a good movie and eat popcorn together. Teach children *how* to choose a good movie the same way you teach them the difference between a good book and a bad one. Go on picnics and ride bikes together. As children grow older, teach them how to play golf, (it's a game they can enjoy into their 90s!) Learn to ski with them or enjoy any of the variety of sports available today. Develop friendships—your friends, your partner's friends, and your children's friends. Have friends for dinner and take time to do things with them. All of these activities help strengthen family ties and are a vital part of our "calling."

The crowning touch of this call is learning the importance of becoming thankful people within our families. I believe an ungrateful attitude is responsible for much unhappiness in today's homes. Karl Menninger asks an interesting question, "Does the sin (or symptom) of ingratitude lie in not *acknowledging* the gratefulness or in not having the feeling?" [12] Have we forgotten what it means to *feel* thankful toward each other today? Do we understand how important it is to genuinely appreciate one another and to treat each family member with gentle kindness and a thankful heart? Sometimes I wonder why we do not show more kindness toward one another. It is so simple to do and means so much. Perhaps we all need to learn to live by the beautiful words in 1 Corinthians 13:4–8:

> This love of which I speak is slow to lose patience—it looks for a way of being constructive. It is not possessive: it is neither anxious to impress nor does it cherish inflated ideas of its own importance.
>
> Love has good manners and does not pursue selfish advantage. It is not touchy. It does not keep account of evil or gloat over the wickedness of other people. On the contrary, it is glad with all good men when truth prevails.
>
> Love knows no limit to its endurance, no end to its trust, no fading of its hope; it can outlast anything. It is, in fact, the one thing that still stands when all else has fallen. (PHILLIPS)

What if each of us lived by our high calling and became God's love in action? We would discover a renewed longing to bring joy, comfort, and protection to our families. In turn, each family member would feel protected and wanted. We would know that we were loved, cherished, and *precious* in the eyes of one another. We would experience the deep contentment which comes from knowing that out of five billion people in the world, there is a loving family unit committed to loving us. That is a comforting thought! As Proverbs says, a good family is "far more precious than jewels." "A loving family is a solid guarantee that no matter what else may happen, at least there will be SOME love in the world."[13]

It is time for us as individuals and as a nation to begin rebuilding our family traditions. We live in a world that is torn by constant strife; filled with both good and evil, ugliness and beauty, war and peace, light and darkness. Yet, in the midst of this chaos, a family can live in peace and trust, free from fear. The home can be a place where all members find comfort in the embracing arms of love. A family is where our love belongs and where our roots lie safe and secure. Mark Twain said, "All we really need is a sound roof over our head, a fire to sit by and a family of our own to love."

The Family

This was God's plan when He created the family. Our calling is to stand strong against the forces seeking to destroy it. God provides all of us with the wisdom, strength, and love to answer that call.

Thought Questions

CHAPTER FOUR

1. Share one or two of your underlined thoughts.

2. List some of the changes you have seen take place within the family structure during the past few years. Why do you think this has occurred?

3. What important values do you find lacking most often in today's families? What can you do to help restore these values?

4. Is it realistic to expect the family to be our top priority in today's busy world? (Share your thoughts and any ideas you have to make the family a top priority.)

5. What difference would it make in your life if you saw your family as a "high calling" from God? What can you do to bring this about?

6. Where is your favorite eating place as a family? What can you do to enhance your mealtime? Why is eating together so important?

7. What can you do to make your partner feel cherished? To make your children feel precious?

8. What do you do for fun with your family? Why is this so important?

FIVE

The Myth of the Super Mom

There is nothing fulfilling about fatigue.

MY DAUGHTER DEBBIE and her family were excited when they found a nice place to rent in a neighborhood with other families. However, their excitement ended when they found out that the lovely neighborhood became a desolate ghost town during the weekdays. All the houses stood forsaken and forlorn. Doors were locked and shades were drawn. Silence reigned supreme. Debbie found herself and her two little boys completely alone during the day. It wasn't long before she was looked to as the "sole mother in residence." Neighbors asked her to keep an eye on their latchkey children after school. If one of them got hurt, Debbie provided a Band-Aid and a kiss. She was given keys to let the plumber in, or asked to "Make sure the television repairman finished his job." Her house became the main depot for various delivery men, especially at Christmastime. This resulted in countless phone calls to inform neighbors that their packages had arrived. The prevailing attitude of the working mothers was, "Well, she's home anyhow and doesn't have anything else to do." Debbie

47

found herself asking the same question that rings out in countless neighborhoods across our land, "Where have all the mothers gone?"

Not long ago women all over the world looked to the American homemaker as the ideal. They thought we were, of all women, most fortunate. We had everything—a home, a husband who took care of his family, and children who respected their parents. We were educated far above the rest of the world's educational standards. We had achieved all of our grandparents' dreams. We had every modern convenience. Women no longer had to slave in the brutal sweat factories or labor in the fields digging potatoes from morning to night. Children did not have to drop out of school at age ten or eleven, as my father did, to help support the family. They could complete high school and often went to college. Children were free to be children. They could belong to Boy Scouts or Girl Scouts, play baseball after school, take music lessons, and go camping during the summer.

The children of the not-so-long-ago past, lived in a home where Mother was always there (not the TV), and where their father returned every night. For a few short years in history we had it all—everything that women in preceding generations longed for, and all that future generations will look back upon as a dream.

It was about then that the woman's movement arrived on the scene and drastically changed our view of the American home. Now millions of women have left their homes and joined the work force. We bought the package that "women have outgrown the housewife role."[1] We were told that man was woman's greatest enemy and that our homes had become nothing more than a parent trap.

As a result the traditional home is often scorned and ridiculed today, and our roles as women are trivialized. Being a homemaker isn't easy. There are times when we feel alone and isolated, as my daughter did in her vacant neighborhood. Many women are ashamed to tell anyone they stay home with their children. They have become "closet homemakers."

The Myth of the Super Mom

Many years ago, the Communist leader, Vladimir Lenin, inadvertently stated the feminist goal by saying, "We cannot be free if one half of the population is enslaved in the kitchen." The modern-day woman's movement picked up on that theme and amplified it to the point where there can be absolutely no equality as long as women are home-makers. Betty Friedan said, "The women who 'adjust' as housewives, who grow up wanting to be just a housewife are in as much danger as the millions who walked to their death in the concentration camps."[2]

When I was a young mother no one told me home-making was an endless drudgery. I didn't know taking care of my family was pointless. I wasn't bombarded everyday by the media showing mothers in and out of neighbors' beds. I never read a book or article decrying the absurdity of femininity. No one belittled my God-given right to raise my children in a home where their father was deeply loved and where everyone found a sense of security. As a home-maker and a mother I had the joy of creating a home and the privilege of shaping a human being.

Today's woman carries a heavy load. She is far from liberated. She accepts the myth that in order to be free she needs to get a job. She leaves her home with stars in her eyes and sets out to live her own life. "I want to live my own life. For whose lives could they live except their own? Everyone must look after something in the world and why were they living their lives if they looked after antique fur-niture, or parrots, and not when they looked after husband, children or grandparents."[3]

The results of this mass exodus from the home is just beginning to be studied. Research shows that it isn't just for economic reasons that mothers have joined the work force. It is estimated that 65% of working mothers live in a home where the husband's income is $35,000 a year or more.

COSTLY GUILT

While recently having lunch with an attractive work-ing mother, I talked with her about the unforseen problems she faced as a new mother with a career. She confided, "No one will ever know how hard it is for me to leave my little baby with a sitter every day. I grew up with my mother at home, and it isn't easy to deal with the daily guilt I feel in working." All over the country mothers are laboring under a dichotomy of guilt that has been thrust upon them. If they choose to stay home with their children, they feel guilty because they are not out in the marketplace, "making a contribution to society." If they choose to have a career, they are inundated with guilt every time they think of their family. They feel guilty for ignoring their children and not being able to find adequate day care. Working mothers feel especially guilty because they are so exhausted at the end of the day. There seems to be no time for their husbands or even themselves.

> Where once we were expected to be at home, today we are expected to be at work. Where once we felt compelled to sacrifice ourselves in the interest of our families, we are now being urged to sacrifice our families while we "look out for Number One."[4]

The mother who chooses to stay home with her children feels guilty for not contributing to the financial needs of the home. She feels guilty because she cannot give her children the many luxuries and advantages they could have if she worked. And she feels guilty because she thinks her working friends look down on her. Society often portrays the homemaker as uneducated, incompetent, and uninteresting.

> They have become dependent, passive, childlike; they have given up their adult frame of reference to live at the lower human level of food and things. The work they do does not require adult capabilities; it is endless, monotonous, unrewarding.[5]

Both the homemaker and the working mother end up feeling totally frustrated and angry as result of this continuous guilt. We are angry at our husbands, our children, our bosses, and yes, even angry at ourselves. We often feel God played a horrible trick on us when He created us female. We have let society push us into choosing sides. The career woman looks down on the homemaker, and the homemaker looks down on the career woman. We have become divided at a time in history when we should be united.

Today's working mother places unrealistic expectations on herself. She is expected to juggle her home, children, husband, and job and do it cheerfully, while being well-groomed in her perfect size-seven figure. She must be intellectually stimulating and always carry with her the newly established symbol of success, her genuine leather briefcase, complete with engraved initials.

> Trying to have it all may not be possible. Achieving a lifelong high-pressure career, raising several children, having a perfect marriage, along with having friends, hobbies, leisure, exercise, health, peace of mind, happiness and financial security seems to be volunteering for over-load in one life time.[6]

A recent Gallup Poll discovered that 66 percent of all Americans now feel it is harder for women to combine jobs and family. Seventy-six percent said it is harder for marriages to be successful, and 82 percent stated it is harder for parents to raise children.[7] We pay a high price for our "liberation." More women go to psychiatrists than ever before. More take tranquilizers. There are more broken hearts, and broken homes than ever before. We have more anger, bitterness, frustration, loneliness, guilt, possessions, more sex with less love. We are told we are liberated, but we know we are empty.

SUPER MOM

The piercing sound of the alarm breaks into the cold, dark stillness. With a sleepy yawn, Sharon reaches over to turn it off. She notes that it is five o'clock, time to get up. Today is her turn to take a shower first, which means her husband can sleep in an extra fifteen minutes. She wonders if Robbie, her little three-year-old boy, still has his sore throat. She hopes not.

After her shower, she runs downstairs to turn on the coffee pot. Yesterday was her husband's day to get things going. It helps to take turns. She finishes dressing and combing her hair by 5:45. "Oh," she thinks, "how hard it is to get everyone up when it is so freezing cold and dark outside." She dreads taking the baby out in the early morning frosty air. "What would it be like to sleep in and let the children play in their warm nighties before breakfast?" she wonders, as she goes into Robbie's room to wake him up.

Breakfast turns out to be the usual rush. Her husband gulps down his coffee and cereal so he can dress the baby while Sharon finishes tidying the kitchen. The baby cries when Daddy tries to take her out of her warm crib. Robbie is cranky and says his throat hurts. He doesn't want to get dressed.

Somehow, they all manage to be in the car by seven o'clock. Does Sharon have the diaper bag and all the necessary things to help her children feel at home during the day? It is a twenty minute drive to the day-care center, if the traffic isn't too bad. Sharon wonders if Robbie will tell the teacher he has a sore throat, or if Tammy will cry again when she leaves. She is wrong on both counts this morning. Robbie cries, and Tammy sits on the care-giver's lap, sucking her thumb. "Well, at least she seems happy," Sharon thinks, as she tries to wave a cheery good-bye to Robbie. He does not want her to leave at all.

Back in the car, she settles down with a deep sigh. Is it really only 7:30 A.M.? How can she be so tired? The traffic is terrible today, and Jim doesn't seem to be in a very good mood. He had been up three times during the night with Robbie. It will be a full day for both of them.

By 5:30 P.M. both of them are back in the car driving to the day-care center to pick up Robbie and Tammy. The traffic is even worse than it was in the morning. Both Jim and Sharon try to make up for it by sharing some of the day's events. However, Sharon longs to put her head back and shut her eyes for a few minutes before she faces the frantic next few hours of dinner, playtime, bath time, and story time. Tammy is happy to see her, but Robbie clearly has a fever. Who can she call to come and stay with him tomorrow?

Dinner is over. It wasn't much really, but she hopes it was nourishing. Jim was such a help. She wondered how she could manage without him. What if she was a single parent? While Jim cleans up the kitchen, she gives the children their baths, feeds Tammy her warm bottle of milk, and thinks about how good it is to hold that precious little body close to her. Jim reads Robbie a story, but he cries when it is time to turn out the light. He isn't feeling good and just wants to be held. It is after nine before things quiet down—just enough time to press her suit for the next day and make out the shopping list. There isn't much time left for Sharon and Jim to be together—five o'clock will come around too soon and another day will begin.

This scenario is played out, in various degrees, in millions of homes every day of the week. What is left after a day like that? Both husband and wife are exhausted, stressed out, disillusioned, burned out, and burned up. Liberated? No! Woman's Lib has become nothing more than woman's fib, and the mental, physical, and emotional cost is high. Women have discovered that "there is nothing fulfilling about fatigue."[8] One working mother told me, "I'm so tired. I can't live like this forever." Another woman said she came home from work with a headache and backache every day. She felt like a robot with no time for herself, her husband, or her children. She was simply too tired to prepare a good dinner and so was her husband. "In fact," she said, "I'm always tired these days and I don't like it. We all deserve a better life than we're having now. I wish I could stay home. Maybe we could get along on one paycheck."

No matter how beautiful a house a double paycheck provides, it often simply becomes a place where we pass one another coming or going, grab a quick bite and change our clothes, or lay our head down at night. Today, a house rarely has a chance to become a home.

No one is capable of meeting the demands placed on today's Super Mom. She is discovering that the sixteen-hour workday and the rush-hour commute are not liberating after all. In the end, she is more disillusioned then ever with herself, her job, and her home. These are not happy days for her or for her family. She has become a prisoner of liberation.

CHILD CARE

There isn't a more heart-wrenching problem facing our nation today than the problem of who will care for the children. In America, more than eleven million children daily are cared for outside the home. Few children are able to cope with the continual stress of being dragged out of warm beds, bundled through the cold, dark streets to a sitters' houses, or day-care centers, only to be separated all day from their mothers.

In today's society we have children and promptly leave them to someone else to bring up. "This year, 1985, nearly half the babies born to married mothers were placed in some form of child care before they were a few weeks old. Their mothers went back to work."[9] Over 50 percent of all children under five live in a home where both parents work. Fifty-eight percent of children, ages six to eighteen, have working parents. In 1990, 75 percent of all preschool children will have a mother who works outside the home. Thirty-eight million children under age ten have working mothers.[10]

More than half of all school-age children go to some form of after-school care arrangement—day-care center, a friend's house, a baby-sitter—or are alone as latchkey children. During the summer they often live with grandparents. For school holidays or sickness, they are alone. *TIME* magazine asks a question we cannot ignore, "What troubles lie ahead for a generation of children reared by strangers? What kind of adults will they become?"[11] *TIME* goes on to say, "Day care is hard to find, difficult to afford, and often of distressingly poor quality. Waiting lists at good facilities are so long that parents apply for a spot months before their children are born."[12]

The Myth of the Super Mom

Good child care can be extremely expensive. A full-time day-care center may charge more than $3,000 a year for each child. A well-trained private baby-sitter can cost as much as $200 a week. After subtracting the high cost of child care from a paycheck, one begins to wonder if a career is really worth it during child-rearing years. Besides being very expensive, the search for qualified care givers is as distressing on the mother as it is on the child. Some children have to adjust to seven or eight different arrangements within a year.

It is difficult for a child to adjust to the rigid daily schedule that must, of necessity, be adhered to in any well-run day-care center. The entire day is regimented and everything is done in a group. There is no time for the joyful spontaneity that is characteristic of little children. Playtime, nap time, color time, sing time, eat time, and potty time are all strictly controlled. But perhaps saddest of all, there is no time to be *special* in anyone's eyes. A teacher at a day-care center told me, "We try to hold each child individually on our lap for at least five minutes every day." But what is five minutes out of eight or nine hours? And often that five minutes is cut short by another child's need.

In our desperation to find someone to care for our children, we often have to settle for less than the best. Some centers I visited were dirty. The toys had not been washed, and the children's diapers were not changed often enough. Many children had runny noses, but no one had the time to wipe them. It grieved me to see the teacher look the other way when an older child hit or pushed a little one. She was too busy attending to other things. I noticed that other care givers were often irritable and indifferent to the children. And some workers were not too clean. I felt sad for a little three-year-old boy who arrived at the center at half-past six that morning. It was nine o'clock and he was still so tired that he just stood alone against the wall. I watched the children go outside for recess. Some of them stood quietly at the cyclone fence, watching the cars go by, hoping one of the cars would contain their mother.

In fact, that seemed to be the children's biggest question: "When is Mommy coming?" They asked this throughout the entire day. If one of the mothers arrived early to pick up her child, I noticed the rest of the children seemed quiet and withdrawn after she left. The continual stress of being separated from both parents all day can be damaging to a small child. A child is incapable of understanding why Mommy is gone so long every day.

One mother I talked to at the day-care center said, "I used to have my little girl at a baby-sitter's house. But one day I went to pick her up and I found her, along with seven other little ones, crowded into a tiny bedroom with a gate across the door. The baby-sitter was in the living room watching *General Hospital*."

Another young mother told me she recently quit her job because every time she dropped her baby off at the sitters, the television was on. And when she picked the baby up at the end of the day, the TV was still on, with a little forlorn group of children sitting on the rug watching it. *TIME* magazine said, "People need a license to cut your hair, but not to care for your child."[13] Yet, it is here, in these crowded nurseries that our little children are getting many of their first and lasting impressions about life. It is here they gather so much valuable information about their world.

Of course I visited some excellent day-care centers. They were clean, well-equipped, served nutritious lunches and snacks, and the children were strictly limited in number so each one had special attention. These were run by professional, deeply committed people. It was a joy to spend the day in these centers, but they are extremely expensive, difficult to find, and even more difficult to get into because of the two-year waiting list.

PROBLEMS OF CHILD CARE

It has been estimated that less than 15 percent of all working mothers are happy with the form of child care they

The Myth of the Super Mom

have. They are desperately seeking a warm, loving, motherly type of person to care for their babies. They discover that most women who fit this description are home with their own children. (A woman is really looking for someone like herself!)

One of life's unexpected and rare surprises is the way a baby becomes completely wrapped around our heart while we're still in the hospital. Most mothers are unprepared for the deep bonding that takes place between them and their babies. Many women think they can have a baby, spend a few weeks at home with it, find a good Mary Poppins nanny, and dash out the door—back to their careers—satisfied that they have produced a baby and fulfilled the life-long dream of motherhood.

Nobody told us about the tight grip of love our baby would tie around our heart. (Our grandmothers could have, but we never asked them.) How are we going to leave this precious baby in the care of someone else for nine hours a day? Some mothers I talked to referred to this as their "daily sorrow."

Another unexpected problem the working mother faces is what does she do when her child is sick? Who is going to take care of the baby? An older child is often left home alone to get well. If the child is little, we end up feeling guilty for taking him or her out of their warm bed and bundling them off to the sitter. We feel terrible that we cannot stay home and read stories to them, or just hold them close. Who is going to take care of the children during holidays and the long summer vacation? We may think that we won't feel guilty for working while our children are in school, but when we look at the heartache of today's teenagers, the untold pressures put on them, the unplanned pregnancies, the many sexually transmitted diseases, the devastating drug and alcohol abuse, plus the teen suicide, maybe we are still needed at home.

Dr. Burton White, of the Psychologist Center for Parent Education, feels that every child, regardless of their age, needs to have love and attention *lavished* on them. No

57

school or day-care center is equipped to give a child this kind of attention. Most parents or grandparents have what Dr. White calls "an irrational love" for the child. They receive "tremendous gratification" in their simple achievements. "Their response to these things, their sharing, their enthusiasm, their excitement, cannot be purchased."[14] This is lacking in most forms of child care.

WHO PAYS THE BILL?

We hear a lot today about how the government should provide the necessary funds for child care. The Marxist solution to children has always been to have the government take care of them. At a conference in Houston, the National Organization of Women called for government-funded, day-care centers around the clock, seven days a week across the country. Society as a whole they insist, should bear the burden.[15] But it has been estimated that it would cost the government (that's you and me) at least $125 a week for each child to provide adequate day care for the children now needing it in our country. With eleven million children in this category today, that would be $1.375 billion our government would have to pay out *each week*. (To put one billion dollars into perspective think of it this way: If you received one thousand dollars a day since the year 1 A.D., you would still have 758 years left to receive a thousand dollars a day!) Where do those who advocate that child care become a public responsibility plan to obtain this kind of funding if not from you and me?

I may be idealistic, but I believe *most* couples could get by on the income of one partner. I saw evidence of this in the many people I interviewed, as well as in my own life. It's true, staying home and seeing our child's first step won't buy us a bigger television set. And we won't have everything we want, but who does? Someone asked the millionaire John D. Rockefeller how much money it took to be satisfied. He shook his head and said quietly, "Just a little more—just a little more."

Families with mothers who quit their jobs to stay home felt that the joy and security of having her home far outweighed the things they could have had if she continued to work. When I asked one young mother why she quit her job that she liked so much, she responded, "Because I love my daughter more." Many times, we are not willing to forgo all the things we think a double paycheck could buy. We think we have to have everything now. We don't want to wait ten years to buy our dream home, because with today's divorce rate, we may not even be together in ten years! We may not be willing to make the necessary sacrifice to live on one paycheck, but we are asking our children to sacrifice something each time we send them to spend their days with a paid care giver. We are asking them to sacrifice something very precious from their few years of childhood. If we choose to have children today, we must return to the basics. It's the *parents* who must sacrifice, not the babies.

THE SINGLE PARENT

A tragic phenomenon occurred across our land that none of us could foresee as women began to leave their homes by the hundreds of thousands to join the work force and as divorce became more acceptable than marriage. The single parent emerged as a class of society and is often referred to by the media as the "New Poor." Statistics point out that 80 percent of all single parents are the result of divorce or live-in relationships. The children are the ones who suffer the most from this unhappy, unplanned development.

Each time I interview a single parent my heart grieves. The heavy load of care they labor under day after day, year after year, was far from any form of liberation they had been promised. There is absolutely no way a single parent can stay home with the children. They must work. The ones I talk to say it takes every ounce of energy to work at their job and care for their children. There is no time left over for friends or outside recreation for most of them. With 5.7 million single working parents today (and the number is growing at an alarming rate), to work or not to work is not a choice. Nineteen percent of all working women are single parents. And one out of every six children under eighteen years old live in a single-parent home. Again the number is increasing daily. For the *single parent* who must work, we as a nation have a responsibility to provide good child-care facilities.

> The rewards for families which have been enriched by women's increased independence stands in stark contrast to the real plight of the revolution's unexpected victims; single mothers with limited skills, many without child support or alimony. Many of them simply drifting into poverty, and their children are at emotional risk, increasingly alone because the traditional framework of family care has been eroded. In some cases there's only a memory to replace it.[16]

Single parents have become the norm in today's society. On any airline during the summer, flight attendants lead a line of little children, like ducklings, onto the plane, off to visit their father or mother for a few weeks. This separation also adds to single parents' biggest problems, loneliness and the feeling of resigned hopelessness.

NO TIME

There are a lot of trade-offs that must be made by the couple and children, when both parents have full-time jobs. Making these trade-offs sometimes creates deep resentments in one or both partners. The by-product of guilt and anger is enormous. Often a feeling of deep resentment begins to grow toward those who said women could do it all. The feminist movement has totally ignored a woman's *need* to have a secure home and a healthy, reliable marriage. Above all, it seems to have been oblivious to her need to be a mother, to nurture her own children, and to be with them.

The father also has a growing resentment toward the unfulfilled promise of liberation that seems to affect every area of his life. He feels that he is nothing more than an intimate stranger to his wife. He has no one to share with. Most women have girlfriends and are accustomed to having friends they can share almost everything with. But usually a man only has this kind of relationship with his wife. And now he does not even have her. He feels alone. He feels deserted, and betrayed. "If the major issue for women is overload—balancing career, relationships, children, home— the crisis for men is loneliness and the loss of women."[17] The confident yuppie father, in his three-piece suit and leather briefcase, often becomes desperate every time he thinks of his children, his marriage, and his home. Does he even have a home? Does he really have anything?

In this "liberated" twentieth century, where both parents work, the average family life is filled with stress and unmet needs. We are no longer our own bosses. We are controlled by our jobs, and the child-care center. We may have that big new house; we may have designer clothes; glamorous vacations; money in the bank. In fact we may have everything, except the one thing money can never buy—time together.

We are really far less liberated than we think.

There is no longer any time to
    pursue outside interests
    read a book
    write
    paint
    knit a sweater
    bake cookies
    make an apple pie
    celebrate an old-fashioned Christmas

No time to
    have the children's friends over after school
    answer the teacher's request for a conference
    attend the children's play during the day
    watch their after-school game
    take them to a birthday party
    have them take music lessons

encourage them to practice their music lesson
hear their cheery "Hi! I'm home!"
greet them after school and listen to them talk
listen to the hurt and frustrations of their day

No time to
develop lasting friendships
be hospitable
visit old and dear friends
grow spiritually
read the Bible
pray
attend a small-group Bible study
teach Sunday school
go to Sunday school
go to church
be aware of God's presence

No time to
listen to the crickets sing on a summer evening
watch a sunset
watch the garden grow
walk barefoot through the soft meadow grass
listen to the bird's song
enjoy the fragrance of a spring morning
run along the stretches of silver sand

No time to
have a candlelight bubble bath
do your nails
shop with a friend
sleep
dawdle
relax
linger in the quietness alone
be serene

No time to
understand the shining beauty of love in marriage
hold hands

be spontaneous
play
ride a bike in the park
go skiing
find inner restoration
talk
be transparent
have romance
be kissed in the warm sunshine
walk hand in hand in the silver moonlight

No time to
be loved and cherished
establish traditions
build a memory
love and cherish

No time to
recapture the innocence of childhood
develop the awe
experience wonder
enjoy the newness
sit in the warm sunshine
listen to the low hum of the bees among the clover
feel the autumn heat
smell the pungent fragrance of fallen leaves
watch the rainbow-tinted clouds sail by
listen to the quiet
drink in the scent of color and sound
absorb the sunshine
feel the wind
be filled with laughter
listen to the singing streams
see the silver ribbon of stars stretched across the heavens

THE NEW TRADITIONAL WOMAN

We are beginning to see a new trend in our country today. A new woman is emerging out of the chaos of the past two decades. She is known as the New Traditionalist.

She is a woman who "is oriented around the *eternal* truths of faith and family. Her values are timeless and true to human nature."[18]

In her search to find something to believe in she has discovered the beauty of creating a more meaningful quality of life for her husband, her children, her home, and herself. This new traditional woman is choosing to stay home with her children. She is carefully considering the opportunities open to her. She chooses the field of homemaking in the same thoughtful way others choose to become a doctor, teacher, minister, or engineer. She chooses this profession not because she has to or because it is expected of her, as was true in generations past, but because she wants to.

There are countless opportunities open to women today. This is the positive side to the woman's movement—women have the freedom to move *out* of the home. And now women all across the land are discovering a far greater freedom—the freedom to move back into the home. Those making this life-changing decision find a whole new support group waiting to cheer them on. Women have learned that life in the marketplace was not as glamorous as was implied, nor was Woman's Liberation very liberating. We have carefully observed what the past twenty years have produced in the way of broken homes, divorce, severed relationships, drugs, alienation from our partner, our children, and from God. The price we paid was too costly.

> A whole new generation of mothers rocks the cradle today. They are savvy to their rights and aware of their choices. And though they have been raised with the notion that a woman's greatest contribution lies outside the home, they are discovering—sometimes to their great surprise—that they want to devote more time to tending the hearth and caring for their children.[19]

PLANNING AHEAD

Women following the new traditionalist role have endless, creative choices. We can do almost anything we want—fulfill any dream—open any door. But we must remember that no door will magically open without the proper key. And the key to any successful venture in life is to *plan ahead*. Without planning, we can do nothing. With planning, we can do anything. We must prepare ourselves for life's various stages.

Before our children are born, we must plan, with our partner, exactly how we are going to live on one paycheck. We must have a plan to meet the needs of the family in case of a prolonged illness, or the death of our spouse. We must know how we would provide for ourself and our children should an unforeseen divorce take place. And we must prepare to help out with our children's college expenses. While our children are growing up we must plan for what we would like to do when they leave the nest. Many women never take these important issues into account and the results can be disastrous.

I am convinced that the secret for a successful life after the children are gone is to begin to plan early. Consider things you would like to do or what you would like to become as many as ten years before the last child leaves home. Then study and prepare to do them. When my daughter was in grade school, the teacher asked each student to write a short paper about their father. One of the things Debbie wrote was, "My dad dreams dreams and he does them." Are you dreaming any dreams today about what you would like to do in the future? Are you "doing" them?

One woman I read about took two classes a year at the community college while her children were growing up. By the time they went off to college, she had a fascinating career in teaching art history. Planning opened a new door for her. During the summer, she and her husband are able to travel around the world and visit many of the historical places she teaches about.

Another creative homemaker chose to study nursing once her children were in school. After they were grown, she not only had a fine profession waiting for her, but she goes to Asia every summer for six weeks and works in a refugee center.

My favorite story is of a woman who studied political science while her babies were growing up. This gave her the intellectual challenge she needed during those years, but more important, she is now an active congresswoman and loves every minute of it. Her children are in college and her husband is tremendously proud of her.

When my last child entered high school, I took a correspondence writing class. I have been writing ever since. I have the joy of seeing my books printed in different languages and sold throughout the world. Being an author has provided me with many unexpected adventures. I have visited fascinating places and met interesting people. But this new and delightful career came about only because I prepared for it while my children were still home.

Another woman I talked to sold her business. She said it consumed all of her time and energy, twenty-four hours a day, and it simply was not worth it. She went on to say, "I'm trading in my leather brief case for an apron, home, and freedom!" She said she wanted the kind of freedom that comes from being home with her children, who were growing up all too fast without her, and with her husband whom she barely knew after twelve years of being "liberated" in the business world. She plans to reopen her business when her children are grown. In the meantime, she will continue to study all the new trends taking place in her field of interest and will dream new dreams.

Not only can the new traditional woman plan ahead for a career, but statistics reveal that it is much easier for a woman to get a good job after the children are gone. Many companies prefer to hire a woman who has raised her family. They find she brings a stable, mature perspective to the marketplace. She is not absent for maternity leave or any of the many childhood illnesses. She brings a sense of enjoyment to her work. She is competent and dependable, and greatly appreciated among her employers and coworkers.

The sky is the limit for the new traditional woman. She has the lasting joy of staying home with her children, but is also free to take art classes, music lessons, go skiing (on a weekday!), play golf, sit by the fire on a snowy day and read a good book, visit friends, and go out for lunch. Instead of taking her baby to the day-care center, she can take the child for a walk in the stroller. The baby has the privilege of hearing mother's voice exclaiming over the pretty flowers, or singing a song as they stroll along. They can stop and watch a mother bird feed her babies. They can be *together* in the daytime! She is free to take her children to the zoo, or go on a picnic on an unexpected sunny day. She can read them stories before they take their nap, or teach them how to count. Most important of all, she can be *with* them.

The new traditional women I meet, who have moved back into the home, are deliriously happy. They love their newfound freedom. Many discover they learn more about their children in the first few weeks they are home than they had the entire previous year. They are ecstatic to take the latchkeys from around the necks of their grade-school children. They no longer have to miss school events. They experience the satisfaction of observing the often ridiculed custom of having chocolate chip cookies, hot from the oven, waiting for their children when they come home from school. And wonder of wonders—they are becoming reacquainted with their husband.

Today, more and more women are finding they made the right decision when they chose the profession of homemaking. They are learning that nothing can replace those years of loving and growing together as a united family. The diapers, the baths, drying little pink toes, and wiping away the salty tears, are exquisite memories that have no substitutes. They now know that the hours spent listening to endless dreams being spun, and sharing the joys and heartaches of family living, come without a price tag.

HOME IS WHERE THE HEART IS

My husband is a busy minister. One of his favorite joys in life is to stay home on a cold, stormy night, and read a good mystery. The first thing he does is to turn on the stereo to some good baroque chamber music. Then he pops a big bowl of popcorn, and builds a roaring fire in the fireplace. However, he must occasionally get up and put another log on the fire or it will die after that first blaze of glory.

This is exactly what happens in our homes. We start off married life in a blinding blaze of romantic love. (God, in his infinite wisdom, knew we could never stay in that state of perpetual bliss or none of us would ever accomplish anything in life!) But marriage is built on something far more stable than the first flash of romantic love. It is built upon the solid foundation of our wedding vows and the commitment we made to one another before God. Because of that, the radiant flame of romance becomes a soft glowing ember that can burn steadily throughout a lifetime. But the embers would die if we didn't continue putting additional logs of love, honor, respect, kindness, and sacrifice on the fire.

We all long for the same thing in life. We want to be loved. We want someone to share that love in a place called home. This is the way God created us. Few things in life are more significant than establishing a godly home.

Our ability to create this kind of a home is the most important thing we can contribute to ourself, our family, and our country. Everything that is of lasting value, springs from a loving, secure home. If that one pillar is solid, we can face almost any other obstacle in life. "A home is where loveliness should spread. They should come to it weary and sickened and go away made new. They should find peace there, beauty and the cleansing of their sins."[20]

Home is a place where people care about you. It is a place that sends each one of us back into the world restored and renewed. It is a place where someone cares enough to rub your aching head at the end of the day and murmur softly, "Oh! Poor baby." (Regardless of age or gender!)

Home is a place we can take refuge in. We can go to it in times of darkness and be soothed. Elizabeth Goudge says, "Every living thing must have somewhere to bolt to." When life is filled with outside pressures, home is a place where we can bolt, in the midst of the storm, and find a core of quietness, tranquility, and warmth. Home is the beloved background upon which all else in life takes place.

Home is a place that is good to you; it is a place of contentment and comfort—the one dear spot on earth. Oliver Wendell Holmes said, "Where we love is home, home that our feet may leave but not our hearts."

Home is a treasured book filled to the last page with dreams that have been spun through the years and memories of shared joys and sorrows. Each page is written with love and with the contentment that comes only from a lifetime together. "A home is built of loving deeds that stand a thousand years."

My young friend, David, wrote the following story. To me, it represents the simple, though profound hopes and dreams of a home and life we all long for. I always read it with a smile—a tear—and yes, a prayer.

My Life With ♡ Jenny

When I grow up I hope
I mairy Jenny Yes I hope
I will.
I will build her a big
  house. she will have
her own room with her and me.
She will love me

at are weding she will get a
beautiful ring.
She will Loave her
home I will be and
artest and everytime
I come home
  she will kiss me.
She will have a
swiming pool and a fouten.

The Myth of the Super Mom

We will have a

grate garden

with roses and
Dafedils and dases
and tooleps.

And a great ~~tidr~~ librery
will elizebeth gooj
and tresure island.

And a grand balkeng

that will make her
look ~~to~~ like a queen.

And she will

Love me very mush.

[20]David Viau, eight years old; Feb. 1985; used with permission.

Thought Questions

CHAPTER FIVE

1. Share one or two of your underlined thoughts.

2. If you grew up in a home where your mother had an outside job, list the positive and negative feelings you had. If your mother was at home during your growing up years, what did you like about that?

3. List some of the problems that confront our children in child care. What can we, as individuals and as a society, do to help?

4. What did you learn about money from your parents?

5. What is your biggest money problem today?

6. Is it possible to live on one salary in today's world? (If you answered no, why? If you answered yes, how?)

7. When must a career homemaker be prepared to step in and help with expenses?

8. What do you think caused the increase of single parents?

9. What can we as a society do to help ease single parents' heavy burdens?

10. Choose a single parent you know to pray for. List some practical ways in which you can encourage him or her.

11. According to this chapter, what is the one thing money cannot buy? Why is this so important in our lives and in our homes?

12. What are you doing to plan ahead for the "empty nest" years?

13. Why do you think employers are seeking more and more to hire women who have raised their families?

14. Describe the new traditional woman.

15. What are some of your dreams?

SIX

Children of Liberation

A child is the beauty of God in this world.

IN OUR COUNTRY, children have often become nothing more than a liability to care for and a burden to bear. We burn them, beat them, choke them, and molest them in alarming numbers. They are a nuisance, a bother, and an expense we could do without. We abuse them sexually, physically, and emotionally. Over two million cases of abuse are reported each year. And the number of unreported cases staggers the imagination.

But perhaps the most troublesome aspect of all is that children demand our time. They are naive enough to expect us to share twenty years of our time with them—something we are no longer willing to give. Think of it! (If we should live to be eighty, we would still have sixty years in which we did not have to care for children.) Another result of the woman's movement is that we have accepted the lie that in order to be liberated, we must be free from the "burden" of bringing up children. "In order to raise children with equality, we must take them away from families and communally raise them."[1]

Are we becoming a nation that no longer likes its children? Ann Landers asked her readers a provocative question that we cannot ignore. "If you knew then what you know now about your children, would you still have them?" Over forty thousand readers responded. Seventy percent said no! Children have become nothing more than an annoying interruption to our lifestyle, and a hindrance in our mad search for liberation. Mothers are no longer willing to stay home and raise children, and fathers no longer want to accept responsibility for supporting them. One young mother of a little two-year-old told me, "If I had to stay home with my baby every day, I would go crazy!" She joined the work force and left her baby in the care of a total stranger.

We know that our children are our greatest natural resource. Then why do we leave them to grow up alone? Prince Albert of England instructed his people to, "Take care of the children and the country will take care of itself." How did we get so far off the track today?

Perhaps we need to observe how the animal world cares for its young. A recent study of monkeys showed that the mother monkey often gives her baby more care than many human mothers give their babies in our culture. The mother monkey never leaves the baby's sight during the day, and the baby remains close to her throughout babyhood.

God greatly honored woman by giving her the privilege of being a mother. The task is totally compelling, extremely complicated, and completed too soon. Mother Teresa reminds us that, "A child is the beauty of God in this world." Has this simple, though profound truth been forgotten in our desire to be liberated?

LATCHKEY CHILDREN

There are over eight million latchkey children, under the age of thirteen, who come home after school each day to nothing but an empty house and a television set. It is impossible to put into perspective what implications this modern-day tragedy means to our country and our children.

Children of Liberation

There is no one to greet these children with a smile and warm hug when they arrive home from school; no one to praise the pretty picture they labored so hard to draw; no one to listen to their intense disappointment at being put into a slower reading group; no one to share the joy of being chosen for the school play. The house is often in disarray due to the frantic scramble of everyone going out the door at the same time in the morning. Unmade beds and dirty breakfast dishes give the entire house an eerie sense of abandonment. These children are repeatedly instructed to pull the shades and keep the doors locked at all times. They are forbidden to answer the door because the media continually informs parents that latchkey children are the latest prey for child molesters. These rules, given by uneasy, worried parents, cause a cold knot of fear to grip children's hearts!

One little ten-year-old girl said she would come home from school and hide under her bed every day until her parents arrived. Can you imagine what goes on in her mind each day while she lies under the bed, straining her ears for every strange noise? Or consider the little boy who would come home from school, set his books on the kitchen table, and open them to the page of his homework. After fixing a snack, he would lock himself in the bathroom for the next several hours. The minute he heard his parents come in, he would open the door, dash to the table, and pretend he had been studying all afternoon. He was ashamed to admit how frightened he was to be all alone in the house. He knew his parents expected him to be "a big man." There are other similar cases; however, most children simply come home, lock the doors, and watch television until their parents arrive. When parents think about what is aired on after-school television, we should be the ones gripped with fear.

We forget how frightening it is for children to be alone in the house day after day, year after year. In later life, many of these children describe their growing-up years as very lonely and fearful.

Latchkey children with younger brothers and sisters to care for have a different set of problems. They may not experience the lonely fear. Instead they are expected to be a surrogate parent to younger sisters and brothers, as well as a part-time housekeeper and cook, all the while trying to grow up in a very confusing world.

Most latchkey children are forbidden to have friends over after school. The reasons for this are easily understood. In fact, one of the main concerns of mothers who stay home is that their children might go over to a friend's house where no parent is present. (Studies reveal that most teenage sex takes place in a home where both parents are working and no adult is home).

Latchkey children who are unable to have friends over and are not permitted to go outside and play experience no bicycle riding, no baseball games, no happy games of hopscotch, and no just "hanging around," talking about the day's events. After sitting in school all day, there is no opportunity to run and play or be with friends. Many children are unable to attend after-school birthday parties because they must hurry home to take care of younger sisters or brothers. These limitations seriously curtail many of their social skills. Much of the enjoyment and playfulness of childhood is stolen from these eight million latchkey children—never to be replaced.

A child who is asked to assume the role of a parent is often deprived of the experience of being a child. One unhappy result is that the child grows up much faster than we may want him or her to. We discover, too often and too late, that our children have been pushed into independent living long before they are capable of it.

The latchkey solution for the working parent usually comes about because the baby-sitter of school-age children gets sick, and the children get along fairly well on their own for a few days. This in turn brings about a sense of false security for both parents and children. Parents think of the money they can save by not having a daily baby-sitter, and the children think they are old enough to take care of themselves. They do not realize at the time, the heavy responsibility that has been laid upon them for years to come. Thus the latchkey child comes into being, and it is nearly impossible to reverse the role once it is tried and successful. Most child experts strongly oppose children being left alone in the house for extended periods of time.

Parents see latchkey children as mini-adults. They expect the children to understand their needs and frustrations as working parents. They want them to know how difficult it is to juggle both a job and a home at the same time. They expect children to be independent and totally reliable at too early an age, often forgetting that the children have needs that can only be met by parents—the warmth and security of a mother who is there, a place of safety to come home to, the symbolic cookies and milk, and someone to share them with. We are living in an illusion if we think things are better today with our big houses, fancy cars, and large monthly mortgage payments, all of which demand two incomes. The sad thing is that no one is home in those big houses, except the latchkey child or children. Because of the many pressures placed upon these children it is easy for them to become apathetic and lose a sense of purpose and meaning. They can easily resign themselves to the fact that this must be the way life is.

We are presently producing a nation of troubled, lonely, unhappy, and angry children. Boredom is often their biggest problem, followed by loneliness and fear. They feel abandoned. They have been forced too soon to deal with broken homes, drugs, sex, both parents working, and continual violence—beginning with the toys in their toy box, and extending to the living room television set. In many instances their lives have become nothing more than an aching void filled with, "abysmal gaps of darkness."[2] Problems that used to be associated with adults have become normal childhood experiences. Today's teenagers are the latchkey children of the early '80s. Can we really blame them for their behavior?

TRADITIONS

Saint Therese Martin, in describing her childhood, once said, "My earliest memories are of smiles and tender caresses." Oh! To make this our children's earliest memories! To help them recapture the magic years of childhood. To provide them with a home that is secure and warm in this cold, uncaring broken world.

When I think back over my childhood, I can rarely remember a day when my mother was not there when I came home from school. She really did have warm German sugar cookies waiting for me, their aroma filling the house with goodness and love. She was there to take me to a birthday party or a piano lesson. She was there to ask me how school went that day. I remember her sitting on the couch after dinner was prepared, listening for Dad's car to turn into the driveway. She would meet him at the door with a kiss every night. I can never remember an exception to this. Our home was a warm, loving place. It was clean, peaceful, and happy. My parents were hand-holding sweethearts for forty-seven years.

Of course they faced problems in their lives together, and my entire childhood was not spent skipping across sunny rainbows. Being a homemaker is not all warm sugar cookies and milk. When we provide a good home, we acknowledge that some chores can only be described as boring and sheer drudgery. Changing diapers and listening to crabby children crying can be hard work and demand endless patience. It is important to accept the negative as well as the positive aspects of being a homemaker. This is true of any career. Still, I cherish the good childhood memories and traditions my parents gave me.

The following is what I had written in my journal the night of my fiftieth birthday.

So many thoughts go through my mind tonight. I think of the beautiful gift of life God has blessed me with these past 50 years. I am especially thankful for my mother and father,

80

and for the happy, loving, Christian home they gave me. It was a secure home where I learned about Jesus—my mother taught me Bible verses, and prayed with my sister and me every night. Our home was open to missionaries from many countries and I have vivid memories of hearing of their adventures and their dedication to the Lord. To grow up in a Christian home with parents who love the Lord and who love each other is the greatest legacy a person could ever receive. How blessed I am. Thank You, Jesus.

We have one childhood to give to our children. Let's do all we can to make sure it is good, rooted and grounded upon the Word of God. We cannot permit those few precious years to slip away. We must take time to love our children. To be with them. This is the "sacrifice of love" we give to them. The results of this sacrifice are passed on to future generations. The traditions we build into our children's lives are the ones that will govern the way they live the rest of their lives. Remember Reb. Tevya, from *Fiddler on the Roof*, when he said, "Because of our traditions, everyone knows who he is and what God expects him to do." Do our children know who they are and what God expects of them? It is in the home where they learn these important truths and are taught commitment, compassion, companionship, and courage, as well as how to receive love and give it away. In the home children practice the eternal principles of moral and spiritual values that will guard them throughout life.

> The joys of motherhood, the fulfillment of a loving home shared with children being shaped and molded into young adults, the comforts of grown children and growing grandchildren enjoyed in the autumn and winter years of life—these are conspicuously absent from the public discourse about women's issues. . . .[3]

Let's take the latchkeys from around our children's necks! Let's unlock their prison doors of "liberation" and set them free to enjoy those few precious years of growing up in the magic garden of childhood. And let's remember that the essence of childhood is the freedom to dream dreams. For only as we grow older can the dreams of childhood emerge and spill into the world, benefiting those far and near.

Thought Questions

CHAPTER SIX

1. Share one or two of your underlined thoughts.

2. What did Prince Albert of England instruct his people to do? Why do you think this statement is so significant?

3. List some of the problems today's latchkey children face? Why is it important for us to understand these problems?

4. Describe a happy memory from your childhood.

5. Share a meaningful family tradition.

6. What value do you cherish most from the training you received as a child?

7. What important moral and spiritual values are you passing on to your children? How are you doing this?

8. How would you like your children to remember you?

SEVEN

Relationships Restored

All of life is an adventure in forgiveness.

AFTER A FRIDAY night conference I spoke at, an attractive young woman named Debbi came up to talk to me. She told me that her husband had broken his neck in a skiing accident a year ago and as a result, he was completely paralyzed. She shared the heartaches and problems the two of them and their two little boys faced during the past year. The words of her story were filled with courageous strength and compassionate understanding. Underneath, was an unshakable faith in God. As we talked she said something I hope I never forget. "God has taught me one thing above everything else this year, and that is that my relationship with my husband is the most important thing in all the world. Not his arms, not his legs—nothing matters, except our relationship with one another."

As I went back to my room that night, her words rang loud and clear through my mind, "Nothing matters except our relationship with one another." Debbi and her husband,

Billy, had learned something most people never learn—life *is* relationships. They learned that the most important thing in the world is not money, not designer clothes, not a big house, not position, or even health. They learned that the most important thing was their relationship to God and to one another. Nothing else in life is of lasting value. God created us as relational human beings. He ordained that we should have an eternal relationship with Him. Saint Augustine expressed it well, "Oh God, our souls are restless until they find their rest in Thee." Jesus summed up everything we need to know about relationships with His profound declaration: "Love the Lord your God with all your heart, and with all your soul, and with all your mind. This is the first and great commandment. And the second is like it: 'Love your neighbor as yourself.' "[1]

God designed us to have an eternal relationship with Him. But he also created us to have deep and lasting relationships with one another while we live on the earth. Debbi and Billy were learning the value of this supreme truth: God created us to need one another. He created us to be dependent upon one another. We cannot live in isolation. We are not "an island unto ourself." There are those in this world who think they need no one. But, of all people, they are the most miserable. Today we are often told that it is a sign of weakness to need anyone but ourself. However, we are discovering that this is not true. We need each other. We need our partner. We need our children. We need our friends. Without relationships there is no meaningful life. "We are born helpless. As soon as we are fully conscious, we discover loneliness. We need others physically, emotionally, intellectually. We need them if we are to know anything, even ourselves."[2]

Each person needs someone to love. We yearn for someone to care about us. We cannot change the way God made us. When God said, "It is not good for the man to be alone," (Gen. 2:18) that is exactly what He meant. If we say we need no one, we are what C. S. Lewis calls a "cold egoist," and are denying the truth. We are dependent upon each other and need one another because that is the wisdom of God's plan for human life.

FORGIVING RELATIONSHIPS

A few years ago these words from the movie *Love Story* appeared on posters throughout the country: "Love means never having to say you're sorry." What an erroneous statement. I have found the opposite to be true. Love means having to say "I'm sorry" in countless ways throughout a lifetime.

If we are going to have any healthy, growing relationships in this world, then we must put those two magical words, "I'm sorry," into our vocabulary and use them often. With these two words comes forgiveness.

Forgiveness is the ointment of love that brings healing to our marriages and to other relationships. Without it, relationships wither and die. It requires humility to ask for forgiveness, and it takes love to forgive. But it is the only pathway to restoration for the broken relationships we all encounter.

God doesn't ask us to ignore the hurt or wrong done to us. He simply asks us to forgive one another. Forgiveness means giving up our right, something today's culture tenaciously holds on to. Forgiveness means giving up our right for revenge or to punish. It means giving up our right to be right. And perhaps most difficult, it means giving up our right to our self. Jesus said, "whoever finds his life will lose it, and whoever loses his life for my sake will find it" (Matt. 10:39). Jesus gave up all rights to Himself when He died on the cross. This was the price He was willing to pay for our forgiveness. What price are we willing to pay to forgive one another? Are we willing to die to our rights in order to bring forgiveness and healing to our broken relationships?

The Bible's good news is the redemptive message of reconciliation and the restoration of broken relationships. Through God's forgiveness—in Jesus Christ's death on the cross—our relationship to him is restored. And through our forgiveness, our relationships with one another are healed.

The essence of forgiveness is the willingness to let go of hurts and resentments. It is the willingness to show compassion and mercy. This is possible because we were shown the ultimate mercy, complete eternal forgiveness, at the Cross. The Bible tells us that those who have been greatly forgiven should be great forgivers. Forgiveness brings new meaning and a sense of adventure to life. Norman Cousins summed it up appropriately, "All of life is an adventure in forgiveness."

WOMAN TO WOMAN

A good place to begin the adventure of forgiveness is in our relationships with one another as women. Whenever a person writes or speaks about woman's liberation, toes are stepped on and someone becomes defensive. A wall of separation springs up and relationships are broken. It is an extremely sensitive subject, and we often take what is said personally.

I believe all of us as women, along with the news media, are guilty of blowing the entire subject of woman's liberation out of proportion. Division reigns supreme among us because we have distorted the truth of God's plan for our lives. "Other women are not the enemy, and men are not the enemy. Distortion of the truth is the enemy."[3]

The majority of the women in this country never supported the radical woman's movement. An ABC poll showed that only 11 percent of women voters call themselves feminists. Yet somehow we have permitted this 11 percent to represent all the women of America. We have been lured into taking sides against one another, and inciting anger among ourselves. If women are going to move forward today, there must be healing among us. We must stop intimidating each other and passing verbal judgments on one another.

> The answer to women's needs today will not be found in dividing into two emotionally charged camps, glaring at one another, finding fault and placing blame. What we need is peacemakers. Not power seekers. The tension of division is destructive.[4]

There isn't a woman alive who will not agree that many good and positive things have come from the woman's movement. Changes have taken place that were absolutely necessary. Negative burdens women have carried for far too many years have been removed. The old idea that a woman should be paid less for doing the same work as a man is totally repulsive and unacceptable to women as it should be to all men. The Constitution provided women with equal rights. Yet only in recent years have we tapped into the resources guaranteed us.

The term feminist has come into disrepute today. We are tired of being labeled. We are not singular. We are many, and have many diverse goals, dreams, and plans for our lives. The feminist, or anti-feminist title, no longer meets our needs. The day we can be represented by one group or label is over—passé. All women must step down from their selectively labeled soapboxes and begin to restore their relationships with one another. There has been enough hurt and anger, confusion and injustice, among us. The days of division are over. The time for healing has come.

RELATIONSHIPS ENJOYED

Nathan has a gentle, creative temperament. He is an artist, architect, interior decorator, lover of good music, and a gourmet cook. To be invited to his cottage for dinner becomes one of life's treasured memories. An "old world" atmosphere greets you when you walk through the door of his cottage, and a quiet feeling of bygone days settles in. Elizabethan music plays softly in the background, and a fire glows in the fireplace. The dark polished wood of his hand-hewn table gleams exquisitely in the candlelight. An old violin surrounded by feathery greens from the woods serves as an idyllic centerpiece.

Dinner is a gourmet delight. And after dinner, Nathan has planned an evening of music. Several guests had been asked to bring music, and a delightful program follows. There are solos, duets, and readings from various poems. During the evening friendships are built into lasting relationships. Each guest leaves with a feeling of contentment and love. Contentment because such a lovely evening can still take place in this cold, suffering world. And love for Nathan, who cared enough to make the happy memory possible.

Today we're too busy to take time to establish relationships. It's true, it takes time and effort to plan an evening like Nathan's and time is the one thing those of us living in this late twentieth century do not have. We no longer have time to develop relationships with one another. As a result, we often end up living in a lonely, isolated world, going our individual ways, needing no one. How easy it is to let life lull us to sleep! Some day we're going to wake up, only to discover it's time to die! "Wait a minute!" We'll cry, "I'm not ready to die yet. I want to enjoy my life—my loved ones—my friends. I want to run barefoot through the meadow! I want to ride my bicycle with the sunlight chasing me! I want to develop lasting relationships with my partner and my children! Wait—wait!" But it's too late. We have wasted our years, satisfied to exist in a world of mediocrity. We forgot to grow, and learn, and taste life. We have become nothing but cold, lifeless statues, when our loving Creator made us to be like a "tree planted by streams of water, which yields its fruit in season and whose leaf does not wither. Whatever he does prospers" (Ps. 1:3). God designed us to be vibrantly alive and growing, flexible and sturdy, giving shade and strength to all who come under our branches for rest and comfort, while being rooted and grounded in the Word of God and in the knowledge of his love.

One of my favorite authors is Elizabeth Goudge of England. She often writes about friends gathering on a Sunday afternoon to read poetry, followed by a good old-fashioned English tea. Today, we need to unlock the heavy door of our self-made fortress and invite people to come in for tea—invite them over for popcorn and then play one of the many enjoyable games that are on the market. We need to look for creative ways to build relationships with our family and friends. We need to challenge one another, stimulate one another, and become interested in each other. God gave us a beautiful world to enjoy. He gave us the ability to create beauty in the way we love and serve one another. He longs for us to lay aside the lethargic indifference that has gripped our relationships for so long. Let's begin to passionately care about life, about our loved ones, and about developing friendships in this day of broken relationships.

THE SEASONS OF LIFE

Ecclesiastes 3 tells us there is a time and a season for everything in life. Just as the four seasons of nature come and go, so our lives have many beautiful changing seasons.

Even though babyhood is very brief, it is the time when the critical foundation of love is laid. Much of the love we will experience in later life is formed during babyhood. It is a time to be cherished by every parent.

Childhood should be a radiantly happy season of life. It usually includes children ages four to twelve. The important disciplines of life are learned during this period and many of us gain our first and lasting impressions of God. Again, childhood is over too quickly and should be enjoyed to the fullest by parent and child.

Most major decisions are made during the critical teenage season of life, between the ages of thirteen and twenty. Decisions like: education; type of occupation; what kind of person we want to become; and what kind of moral and spiritual values we want—values that will carry us through the remaining sixty-odd years of adult life. Studies reveal that 95 percent of people will choose what part God is going to play in their life before reaching the age of twenty.

The young adult season, ages twenty-one to thirty, is vitally important. Those who have chosen to go to college or graduate school have usually completed their education. They have entered into their field of work. For many young adults, this season of life is crammed full with a job, marriage, establishing a home, and starting a family.

The years between thirty-one and forty are often a season of career satisfaction and promotions. It can also be an important time to stop and reevaluate life, and redirect it if necessary. For the woman who has chosen to be a full-time homemaker, these are years of great pleasure and personal growth. Toward the middle of this season comes the challenge of beginning to prepare for what she would enjoy doing when the children are gone.

The season between forty-one and fifty can be the most fulfilling and productive years, if we have properly prepared for them. They are often years of great personal satisfaction.

However, life's truly golden season is from fifty on up! This is often a period of great joy. It is when many become grandparents—one of God's special gifts to the human race. If our partner is still living, it can be a time when our love for one another takes a giant leap forward. We begin to realize, in a new way, just how precious we are to one another. The vibrant, romantic glow of love from earlier days is often renewed, only this time it has all the deep trust that only comes from years of commitment and loving together.

God expects us to stop from time to time during the seasons of life and take account of where we have been and where we are going. When I look back over my years of married life, I am thankful for the time spent staying good friends with my husband. The memories that stand out most vividly are the times of joy I brought to my family. I am thankful for each moment I spent with my children, teaching them how to experience life in all of its wonder and beauty. I am especially thankful that as a little child of ten, I chose to give my life to Jesus Christ, my great Redeemer, Savior, and friend. And I am thankful for God's continued, unconditional love for me and each person in this world. I revel in the truth that, "God does not love us because we are valuable; but we are valuable because God loves us."[5]

What is a human being? One who is created in the image of God. Much of our humanness is determined by our relationships . . . our relationship to God and our relationships with one another . . . by the way we love and care for one another. "Someday, after we have mastered the winds, the waves, the tides, the gravity, we will harness for God the energies of love; and then, for the second time in the history of the world, we will have discovered fire."[6]

Thought Questions

CHAPTER SEVEN

1. Share one or two of your underlined thoughts.

2. Why are relationships so important to us?

3. What role does forgiveness play in our relationships with others? With our partner? Our children? What is the most difficult aspect about forgiveness?

4. Explain the phrase, "All of life is an adventure in forgiveness." In what ways have you found this to be true in your life?

5. List the positive aspects of the women's movement during the past twenty years.

6. How can we begin to restore the broken relationships between the various women's groups in our country? Why is this so important?

7. How do friendships enrich our lives?

8. Describe a memorable time shared with a friend or friends.

9. What can we do to reach out more to others with the gift of friendship? Ask God to show you someone who needs a friend.

10. What do you enjoy most about the season of life you find yourself in now?

11. What memory stands out most vividly from the season of life you just completed?

12. List two ways you are preparing for the next season of your life.

13. Write a paragraph summarizing your thoughts on Part One of this book.

PART
TWO

OUR
IMPRISONED
SOCIETY

"If there is no God,
all things are permissible."

FYODOR DOSTOYEVSKI

EIGHT

Divorce

Don't sacrifice the permanent on the altar of the immediate.

THE "GREAT SOCIETY" of the '60s has become the imprisoned society of the '80s. Moral and spiritual values have vanished in a permissive puff of smoke. We are in danger of becoming a morally vacant people. Common goodness is nearly nonexistent in many areas of life, and our decaying culture is being sucked into a quagmire of depravity. We have become desensitized. What is most devastating is that we have removed God from the center of the universe and replaced Him with ourselves. We have "exchanged the truth of God for a lie, and worshipped and served created things rather than the Creator" (Rom. 1:25).

Nothing of value has much meaning today. Marriage, the home, family, children, and even the sanctity of human life has been devalued. Each person has been "liberated" to do what is right in his or her own eyes. As a result, we live in a world that is going mad with destructive immorality. We desperately need what Elizabeth Goudge calls, "a change of taste."

As you read through Part Two of this book, I hope you will be challenged to rise in anger and indignation against the debilitating events taking place under the guise of liberation.

DIVORCE

My friend shared with me the following heartache that she has carried with her for over twenty-five years.

"I was only six years old when my parents got divorced," she said in a quiet voice. "I remember I cried myself to sleep every night. No matter how hard they tried to explain it to me, I grew up never understanding why it happened. Now I'm married to a wonderful man. I have two beautiful children. But still, there is an emptiness in my life, a void, an ache, that I just can't seem to fill. I think it's because I know I must go through life never knowing the closeness I could have had with my own parents. I'll never know the warmth and love that could have been mine."

Divorce is a way of life at the end of the twentieth century. It is the accepted and inevitable conclusion to marriage. It is considered normal, not necessary. Every person reading this book has been touched, in some way, by the deep and painful scars of divorce. Nearly 50 percent of all marriages in this nation end in divorce. In Seattle, six out of every ten marriages end in divorce. And if we think second marriages are happier we're wrong! Two-thirds of all second marriages end in divorce. Some divorces are necessary, but less than 5 percent fall into this category. Maybe more couples would stay together and work through their differences and problems if divorce was not so easy.

As a minister, my husband hears many couples' heartbreaking stories. However, some of the reasons people give for breaking up their marriages and destroying their families are incredulous. "She doesn't stimulate me anymore," one middle-aged husband said in all sincerity. Or, "All my growth and creativity have stopped since I married him." Or again, "There is no challenge left in our life together." Such statements remind me of Adam when he told God in the Garden of Eden, "The woman you put here with me— she gave me some fruit from the tree, and I ate it."[1] Adam blamed his wife for his unfortunate circumstances, and we continue to do the same today. Throughout thousands of years of civilization, we still blame the other person.

We live in a disposable culture. We dispose of our spouses, our children, and even our grandchildren, with nonchalant regularity. One husband told his wife over morning coffee, "I want out of this marriage. I have never been happy in it, and I have never loved you!" With that, he left his lovely wife of thirty-two years, his children, and his grandchildren. Several months later, his little grandson, who adores both grandparents, asked in total perplexity, "Grandma—when is Grandpa going to come back and live in this house again?" The trauma of divorce touches every person in the family, to the third and fourth generations.

The tremendous pressure on today's families as a result of divorce is catastrophic. In 1950, very few children grew up in a home where divorce occurred. Today, it is hard to find a child who lives in a home where both biological parents are still in their first marriage. "The majority of children in the 1980's now live in a household in which one or more of the following social conditions exist; divorced separated or single parents; dual-career parents; or a parent living with a mate outside of marriage."[2]

Government statisticians tell us that half of all this year's marriages will fail. The Step Family Association of America says that thirteen hundred step-families are formed *every* day in our country. The ramifications of this fact are many and frightening. We gloss over the emotional scars divorce leaves on both adults and children. We assuage our troubled minds by reasoning that children are better off living in a home where they never hear their parents argue. However, just the opposite is true. Most children prefer to listen to their parents argue than to have them get a divorce.

One tragic consequence of the liberated divorce system is the sudden rise in the number of single parents, and the untold suffering that status entails. Seventy percent of today's families headed by females are on welfare. In America, one out of every six children under eighteen years old lives in a single-parent home. "In the period of 1980–2000, the number of female headed families will increase to more than five times the rate of husband-wife families."[3]

> A community that allows a large number of young men to grow up in broken families, dominated by women, never acquiring any stable relationship to male authority, never acquiring any set of rational expectations about the future—that community asks for and gets chaos, crime, violence, unrest, disorder . . . that is not only to be expected; it is very near to inevitable.[4]

The divorce rate has more than doubled since 1968. And we must ask ourselves why?

ILLUSIONS OF DIVORCE

Peggy and I had gone through school together. I always considered her my most "glamorous childhood friend." We made arrangements to have lunch together on a recent trip to my hometown. I soon learned that life had not been kind to her in the intervening years, even though she was now a top executive. The lines on her face were bitter and care-worn. She told me about the divorce she had initiated fifteen years earlier. When the divorce became final, she was left with the house and three little children to bring up alone. She concluded her story by saying, "If I had known how lonely divorce was, I would have worked a lot harder to keep my marriage together."

We have glamorized divorce today—making it the solution to all our problems and the material for cute movies and amusing soap operas. The media often portrays divorce as a liberating and exciting adventure. I have found the opposite to be true. Instead of the promised glamour and excitement, divorced people often find themselves locked in a tight prison of loneliness and self-imposed guilt, failure, loss, and rejection.

Perhaps one of the cruelest illusions foisted on society is the no-fault divorce law that was supposed to bring true liberation to all concerned. However, it has only been a huge asset to this country's divorced fathers. In many cases these men are no longer legally responsible to support their wives or children. We forgot to count the cost of no-fault divorce in our search for liberation. We did not understand the economic problems this policy would create for the family, and the entire nation . . . until it was too late. "The poverty issue . . . would disappear almost entirely with the improved economy, except that the rates of divorce and the formation of single parent households remain high."[5]

Our liberated divorce laws failed to bring the freedom to society they were supposed to bring. Instead, they trapped millions of people on the merry-go-round of marriage, divorce, and remarriage. Aldous Huxley summed up our permissive stand on divorce when he predicted in his book *Brave New World* that "some day marriage licenses would be sold like dog licenses, good for a period of twelve months, with no lawsuit against changing dogs or keeping more than one animal at a time."

No-fault divorce has become a never-ending struggle for most divorced women. They find it difficult if not impossible just to keep their head above water. One woman told me, "I never dreamed it would be so hard or that I would feel so forsaken. I can barely pay the rent, or the many other bills it takes to run the house. And worst of all, the children and I are left without any medical insurance." Our country is faced with a burgeoning segment of poverty-stricken single mothers. Many ex-husbands feel it is morally acceptable not to support their children. Statistics show that 50 percent of divorced fathers do not pay what they owe their families, and 24 percent pay nothing. That means that *every* day over two million fathers steal from their children. Much of this is due to the loud cries of the feminists, who insisted that, contrary to God's plan, women could provide for all the needs of their families. It is an undisputed fact that when a woman with children is divorced, she is faced with an immediate 73 percent drop in her standard of living. While at the same time, the husband averages a 42 percent *increase* in his standard of living![6]

We are, without a doubt, prisoners of liberation.

CHILDREN OF DIVORCE

Children are always the saddest victims of divorce. Our liberal laws permit a divorce to parents who can no longer get along with each other, even though recent studies reveal that divorce is intensely harmful to children. "Children of divorce have lost something very precious, and they may spend their lives trying to get it back. The damage of divorce is much more than we first thought, and it can last all the way into adulthood."[7] Divorce emotionally scars every child. Outside of the death of a parent, divorce is the most painful experience a child will ever have to face. This is because, "To children, the voluntary separation of parents seems worse than death precisely because it is voluntary."[8] Because divorce is something parents choose to do, it is increasingly difficult for a child to comprehend.

Most children of divorce carry deep yearnings, even into adulthood, that reconciliation between their parents will take place. Many parents think that getting married again will help the children accept the situation. But remarriage actually shatters the children's last ray of hope that their parents will ever get together. This can be devastating for children to deal with, and a period of profound grief often follows. Many children feel they are to blame for their parents' divorce. As a result, they feel it is their sole responsibility to keep a good relationship with the remaining parent—there is a dreaded underlying fear of possible total abandonment. The loss of belonging is often the effect of divorce on children.

One little six-year-old boy said, "I can't see my mom and dad at the same time anymore." Another girl described her parents' divorce as, "It's a scary time." One little girl simply said, "It's sad." A little nine-year-old boy was overheard saying, "Now I have eight grandparents instead of just four. I get lots of presents." Lots of presents seems to be the payoff for children of divorce.

Stress is another result of divorce on children's lives. The added stress of worry and an intense fear of failure in relationships with friends often follows children into adulthood. Girls from divorced homes in the thirteen to seventeen age group exhibit much lower self-esteem and are far more sexually active than girls who come from two-parent homes. Boys carry deep unmet longings for their fathers. Perhaps the two strongest stress-related feelings are rejection and depression. It takes many years for these feelings to be healed. Children of divorce often grow up with an extreme fear of marriage because they know, first hand, the agony and scars they have been left with.

Judith Wallerstein, the executive director of the Center for The Family in Transition, says that 37 percent of the children from divorced homes were more emotionally troubled five years after the divorce than they were when it first happened.

Children never entirely recover from the breaking of their parents' marriage bond. The lonely bewilderment never completely vanishes. It haunts them the rest of their lives. They may not understand the cause, but it is there nevertheless. There are no mooring ropes to give them an anchor in this restless, changing world of liberated divorce.

Every precious baby brought into our world is due a mother and a father—a father who is the guardian, protector, and provider and a mother who nurtures, comforts, and loves. Home should be a place where a little child can dream pleasant dreams at night, beneath warm covers, safe and secure, loved and protected. Yet many children today lay in darkened rooms weeping tears of emptiness into their pillows, longing for someone they once had.

NEW TREND

The day is coming when more and more couples will begin looking for positive and creative ways to save their marriages. I talked to a woman in her early fifties who had gone through the rigors of three marriages and had brought up three sets of children, "his-hers-and-ours." She concluded by saying, "I realize now that I could have been happy with each of my husbands. Most of our problems could have been solved if either of us had just taken the time to work them through. It was too easy to get a divorce. We didn't care enough to fight for our marriage."

> If you're going to fight, fight for the relationship, not against it. Fight for reconciliation, not for alienation. Fight to preserve the friendship, not to destroy it.
> Fight to win your spouse, not to lose him/her.
> Fight to save your marriage—not to cash it in.
> Fight to solve the problem, not to salve your ego.[9]

Let's fight to keep our marriages radiantly alive! Let's not permit ourselves to mention the word divorce. It is taboo. Agree to that before getting married. Mentioning the word divorce can bring a death knoll to a marriage. Any marriage, no matter how good, could end in bitterness and divorce if we let it go. We must care enough to fight to save it—to work things out. "If two people want to rebuild (their marriage), if they want badly enough to love again, they can."[10]

Let's agree not to sell our marriages short. Remember the Old Testament story when Esau sold his birthright for a pot of stew? (Gen. 25:29–34). This birthright was a sacred inheritance passed on from generation to generation. Yet he sold it for a pot of stew! How many of us are selling our marriages, the inheritance of our children and grandchildren? How many of us are sacrificing the permanent on the altar of the immediate?

> Destruction of family life not only kills the beauty of two generations enjoying and understanding each others tastes, and talents, but it robs people of the richness of three and four generations adding to each others knowledge, and the understanding of history.[11]

THE TAPESTRY OF LIFE

While visiting Hong Kong a few years ago, my husband and I went to a factory that is world renown for weaving beautiful tapestries and rugs. The finished rugs are found in the Taj Mahal and opera houses around the world, and their tapestries adorn the palace walls of kings and queens. Inside the factory, each worker sits on a high stool and weaves a tapestry that is rolled onto a large scroll. The work is extremely intricate. Each thread is woven with artistic precision. The colors are rose-pink, amethyst, and dove-gray mingled with midnight blue, amber-gold and the pastel colors of the rainbow. As we watched, we noticed no pattern or design emerging from their work. We mentioned this to the weaver and his face lit up with a ready smile. He explained that a tapestry is always woven from the wrong side. Then he turned the scroll around to the right side of the tapestry. When he turned it over, our hearts caught in wonder at the sight before us. Each thread had been woven to form a design of exquisite beauty. This tapestry was destined to become an irreplaceable treasure, like a supremely valuable precious jewel.

As we walked away from the factory, I found myself thinking that each of us is a tapestry. The great weaver is God. As we watch Him work on our tapestry, we notice how carefully He chooses the colors. We see how the threads of emerald, turquoise, and ruby red are woven joyfully through times of happiness. Then we see Him gently pick up the dark, cold colors of sorrow and despair, cautiously weaving them through the quiet opal-tinted colors of tranquility, gentleness, and serenity. Each thread is woven with eternal love into an intricate pattern of perfection. Someday we will see it from the right side and understand that the tapestry of our life has become one of indescribable splendor—destined to become an irreplaceable treasure, to be enjoyed by our loved ones for generations to come.

What is being woven into our culture's tapestry today? I believe, as a nation and as individuals, we are tired of only seeing harsh, black threads of permissive immorality and broken relationships. We long to see warm, golden colors of love and truth, honor and integrity woven back into the American tapestry of life, with God, the great weaver, designing a pattern of incomparable beauty and glory, that will adorn the walls of our nation for future generations.

Thought Questions

CHAPTER EIGHT

1. Share one or two of your underlined thoughts.

2. Why do you think there are more divorces in our country than in any other country in the world?

3. List some of the consequences of our liberated divorce laws.

4. In what way has divorce touched your life? What can you do to help a friend who is going through a divorce or who is considering a divorce? What can you learn from their experience?

5. In your opinion, what makes a good marriage work? List several ideas.

6. What would you like to see happen in your marriage during the next six months? What do you plan to do to bring this about?

7. What advice would you give to a couple about to be married on how they can keep their marriage alive and growing?

8. What do you feel God's intention for marriage is in light of the following verses?
Matthew 5:31–32; 19:3–9; Mark 10:2–12; Luke 16:18; 1 Corinthians 7:10–17

9. What do you see being woven into the tapestry of your life at this time? Can you describe the colors being used? Would you make any changes? If so, what? Why?

NINE

Pornography

Pornography is not harmless, it is deadly.

O NE OF THE MOST crushing disasters our country has ever faced was the Great Depression in 1928. Banks closed, businesses failed, and people lost their entire life savings. Unemployment was rampant and poverty covered the nation like a heavy blanket. The nation was faced with a debilitating economic paralysis that lasted for over ten years. It was a bitter time, and we still look upon that period with concern and fear, hoping it will never happen again.

However, I believe our nation has entered a second great depression just as devastating as the first. We are in the grips of a moral depression that is quickly becoming the dark night of the American soul.

I am referring to the evil, dehumanizing pornography that is saturating our country. It screams at us from nearly every newsstand, drugstore, and grocery store and has become as natural for us to buy as a quart of milk. It is delivered to our homes, unasked for, through the United States Postal Service. (Even though it is completely against the law.) It has been rightly said that, "Pornography is no longer downtown—it's downstairs."[1] It's not only downstairs, but as close as the nearest telephone. Dial-A-Porn has become the latest in our mad rush for total liberation. Any child in America can pick up a phone and listen to graphic sexual talk. The inner corruption of this evil blight upon our land beckons to us and our children from literally every walk of life. We are told there are more pornographic bookstores in our beautiful country than there are McDonald hamburger restaurants![2]

We live in a sex-soaked culture. Things that were unthinkable a few years ago are now welcomed entertainment. We call it the sexual revolution, but a more accurate name would be the sexual holocaust. In our country over one million children between the ages of four and sixteen are involved in the production of obscene movies and magazines. The Los Angeles police department says that over thirty thousand children, most of them under the age of five, are used each year for pornography. (Lance Morrow, in TIME magazine) "About 600,000 children are exploited each year for money by pornography."[3] And "In 1983 as many as three hundred thousand children, and probably many more, from sixteen to less than six months old are filmed or photographed while being raped."[4] Imagine what that number currently is in this rapidly growing industry!

Our nation's sex crimes have soared during the recent years of liberated pornography. Rapes and prostitution have increased by 80 percent. Studies prove that four times as many sex crimes are committed in areas near adult bookstores and x-rated theaters, yet pornography proponents insist that there is no relation between the two. It is an affront to our intelligence to be told that pornography has no affect on the violent crime that is sweeping this nation.

Pornography is the new frontier to explore and exploit in the name of liberation. It is the invention of totally deprived minds. Based on the dehumanization of women and the ridicule of the family, it represents the total absence of equality between men and women. Today our culture prohibits the exploitation of race, creed, color, and religion, so only two groups are left to exploit, women and children.

A recent Harris Poll showed that 76 percent of Americans want pornographic material outlawed. The Gallup Poll found 85 percent favor tougher anti-smut laws. Why are we allowing 15 to 20 percent rule our culture in the area of pornography? We are constantly bombarded with claims that any kind of restraint on pornography is a violation of the Constitution. This is proclaimed as the absolute truth across this nation, when in fact just the opposite is true. The U.S. Supreme Court has held that obscenity is *not* and never has been protected by the First Amendment. In the Roth vs. United States case, the Supreme Court declared that "the First Amendment guarantee of free speech has never applied to obscene material. The court held that obscenity is not within the area of constitutionally protected speech or press." It is true that today's learned judges have difficulty defining obscenity, yet any nine-year-old child could tell them.

Why do we permit this barbaric evil to inundate American culture? For one reason only. Money! Money is the absolute bottom line of this slimy, filthy industry. Pornography has become an eight billion dollar-a-year business. In 1978, *Forbes* magazine estimated that pornographers took in $16,438,000 *a day*! More recent estimates claim that gross sales reach at least eight or nine billion dollars a year. The child pornography industry alone is a two to three billion dollar-a-year business.

WOMEN AND CHILDREN

Our society is wallowing in a prison of liberated depravity.

> The smut assaulting our sensibilities today capitalizes on violently explicit depictions of sexual acts—heterosexual, homosexual, bisexual. It includes portrayals of orgies, incest, bestiality, sadomasochism, bondage, necrophilia, sodomy, even blueprints for raping women with everything from loaded guns to cucumbers and beer bottles.
>
> If these descriptions shock you as an adult, imagine the effects upon the emotional development of children.[5]

Every kind of sexual perversion is permissible in our country today: men and women having sex with animals, women being tortured and beaten, even murdered and then raped. Robert Stoller has said that all pornography has its roots in hostility. Even the more militant feminists say pornography is a conscious assault against women. Not only are magazines sexually explicit, but they exhibit inhuman cruelty. One showed a woman being held down and raped by a shark. Another featured an advertisement of a young nude woman with a mastectomy. "Missing something? Don't settle for half the fun!" This in spite of the fact that ninety thousand American women get breast cancer every year. Such examples show an obvious contempt for women, and the total insensitivity of the people in this business. Pornography always leaves a trail of sick, depraved men; and exploited, battered, bruised, and broken women.

But in our liberated pornographic society, sexual child abuse is the most despicable example of this grotesque perversion. Wickedness, sin, violence, and destruction are poured out upon children in the name of liberation. Every month over 300 different child-pornography magazines are sold in this country. Anyone can buy from public newsstands magazines with such titles as *"Lolli-Tots," "Baby Sex,"* or *"Chicken Supreme"* and others too disgraceful to mention. These magazines show explicit sex between adults and little children.[6]

"Police vice squads report that 77% of molesters of boys and 87% of child molesters of girls admitted trying out sexual behavior modeled by pornography."[7] The Justice Department estimates over four thousand children in our liberated country are sexually abused and then murdered each year. One doctor has said that he could "cure the venereal diseases, put ointment on wounds and stitch up the laceration, but he cannot touch the damage and scars that have been inflicted on the minds and hearts and spirits of these little ones."[8]

If magazine publishers showing sexually abused children become overnight millionaires, then what is there to say except for what is already being said in the name of freedom: "If it makes me happy looking at such pictures, then it's all right for me. If it doesn't make you happy, then you don't have to buy it." But what about the children portrayed in these magazines? Where is their happiness and rights? What kind of anguished prison of darkness will they be held captive in for the rest of their lives?

With the increase of child pornography, our nation is drowning in a cesspool of sensuality. By our example we have taught this generation of young people that sexual perversion is normal. Pornography is geared toward the teenage boy and young married man, who are the fathers and future fathers of the United States. Through liberated pornography, we have taught them that it is all right to be cruel to women and children and to treat them as mere objects. Women and children can be used and abused with a clear conscience because they must deserve such treatment or it would not be permitted. Pornography dehumanizes the family and ridicules the values that made our country great. We have taken God's design for sexual expression within marriage and turned it into a nine-billion-dollar-a-year money-making business. We have dragged it through the sewer of filth, lust, distortion, and violence—plunging our society into an abyss of total depravity. The dust of death has been sprinkled over us. We are heading for a disaster that will leave its putrefied fallout over our nation for generations. Pornography has become one of the most disastrous sources of evil in our nation today. Nietzsche once stated that "the decay of culture meant not only the decay of man in this culture but the decay of man simply."[9] When any segment of human life no longer holds any dignity, the value of all life is drastically altered.

UNSEEN DANGERS

Pornography is like a drug. It becomes a subtle sexual addiction. The more people see it, the more they want to see it. Ninety percent of those who buy it go back for more again and again. It isn't long before they crave more bizarre and deviant material. Soon, the amount of stimulation is not enough to satisfy. Eventually they become obsessed. Their minds, emotions, and spirits become stunted and poisoned. They end up locked in the tight grips of depravity with no way out. Ultimately, their inner beings are destroyed. Their hearts and souls become corrupt. Things that were once abominable and unheard of are now totally acceptable and even desired. They are alone and lost. Tolstoy described their bitter state well when he talked about Napoleon. He said, "Napoleon lost the power to even think a decent thought." This is the brink of despair upon which America now stands.

CREATIVE ACTION

When society puts a stamp of approval on pornography as it has today, we are in grave danger of losing our humanness. The time is long past when we must "open our eyes and realize that, like air pollution and water pollution, moral pollution affects us all."[10]

The potential for moral pollution begins the first time we indulge in pornography. Do you remember the scene from *The Trial of Nurenberg*, when the judge, played by Spencer Tracy, faced the prisoner, Burt Lancaster, for the first time? The prisoner put his head in his hands and said in a broken, husky voice, "I never realized it would come to the horror of the holocaust."

Tracy responded, "Yes you did—you knew it the first time you signed the paper for an innocent person to be killed." So it is with us. We know that the first time we purchase a pornographic magazine, total addiction lurks just around the corner.

The time has come to face the truth that "pornography is not harmless, it is deadly."[11] We must take an active stand against it by demanding that the current laws are enforced. In addition, we have a responsibility to study and become aware of the depth of the moral lassitude that is sweeping our land, as well as the lasting implications it has on our lives, and the lives of our children. Moral and spiritual values *must* be adhered to. "A society with no shared values including moral values, is no society at all."[12]

Current federal laws could close down the entire pornography business within one year. But we are content to sit back and do nothing. Albert Einstein said long ago, "The world is too dangerous to live in, not because of people who do evil, but because of people who sit and let them do it."

Dostoyevski has been proven right over and over when he said, "If God does not exist, anything is permissible." The graphic results of that truth are evident in our liberated sexual revolution. By making a mockery out of God's laws we are on dangerous ground. "Do not be deceived: God cannot be mocked. A man reaps what he sows" (Gal. 6:7).

Thomas Jefferson summed it up wisely when he said, "Indeed, I tremble for my country when I reflect that God is just, and that His justice cannot sleep forever."

The time has come, indeed is past, when we must gather together as a nation to fight this deadly war that seeks to destroy us. We must return to God, our great Creator, Redeemer, and Savior, and live our lives according to the beauty of his plan. We must constantly bear in mind that we are created in the image of God. And the moral and spiritual values God has placed within each of us are a vital part of that image. This is the everlasting heritage God has granted each of us. We must band together as a nation— agreeing that we will not rest until this dreadful scourge of pornography is eliminated.

The following is a moving story told by Holocaust survivor and Nobel Peace Prize winner, Elie Wiesel.

> A just man comes to Sodom hoping to save the city. He pickets. What else can he do? He goes from street to street, from marketplace to marketplace, shouting, "Men and women, repent. What you are doing is wrong. It will kill you; it will destroy you." They laugh, but he goes on shouting, until one day a child stops him. "Poor stranger, don't you see it's useless?" "Yes," the just man replies. "Then why do you go

on?'' the child asks. ''In the beginning,'' he says, ''I was convinced that I would change them. Now I go on shouting because I don't want them to change me.''[13]*

Let's never stop shouting!

*See note 14 for addresses and information on what you can do to help fight pornography.

Thought Questions

CHAPTER NINE

1. Share one or two of your underlined thoughts.

2. Why do you think the author used the example of the Great Depression in describing pornography?

3. What is the bottom line of the pornography industry?

4. What main audience is pornography geared toward? Why does this pose such a serious threat to our nation and to our families?

5. List some of the dangers we face as a nation and as individuals due to the widespread use of pornography.

6. How would you explain the dangers of pornography to your children?

7. Why is it important that we never "stop shouting"?

8. Can you think of any creative action you can take as a stand against pornography?

9. What did you learn from this chapter that you were not aware of before?

TEN

Abortion

Civilization is another word for respect for life.

AFTER A LONG, yet fulfilling day of speaking, counseling, and praying with those who had needs, I found myself looking forward to returning to my cabin to be alone and quiet. But when I opened my cabin door, a young woman in her late twenties was waiting for me. I'll refer to her as Sherry. As we began to share together, she said in a quiet voice, "Seven years ago I did something so terrible that I know I will never be forgiven." She didn't say what it was and I didn't feel free to ask. However, I reminded her of some of the things I had mentioned in my talk about God's forgiveness. I reassured her that regardless of what she had done, God loved her with total, unfailing love; that when Jesus cried out from the cross, "It is finished!" that was exactly what He meant. The penalty for sin had been paid for all time and eternity; His love for her was unconditional; and His forgiveness was complete. When she grasped this magnificent truth and received God's loving forgiveness for whatever she had done, tears of relief filled her eyes.

The cabin became filled with a great quietness as the peace of God began warming her troubled heart. There was only the ticking of the clock. Then I asked if she had ever asked the person she had hurt to forgive her. A long pause of silence followed, broken only by her quiet weeping. Suddenly

121

she cried out in a loud tormented voice, "I can't ask them for forgiveness, because—Oh, God!—they aren't here!" A long shuddering cry of hopelessness filled the little room. Then, in a hushed whisper, she said, "I killed my baby. . . . I had an abortion." Total silence fell upon the room. Then the air was split with the most heart-wrenching cries I have ever heard. "O, God! . . . Oh, God! . . . I killed my baby!"

As I held her in my arms, a heavy sadness filled my heart, and we cried together for her lost baby and the twenty-five million other aborted babies in our country. I wished those who had so "liberated" women to have easy abortions could have listened to the cries of seven long years of agonizing grief and guilt.

I knew that more healing and forgiveness needed to be dealt with if Sherry was to be completely free. After she stopped crying, she brought up one of the areas. In a quiet voice she said, "I know when I get to heaven some day, my baby will hate me for what I did."

Then it was my turn to do something I had never done before. After expressing a silent word of prayer, I began to share with her a beautiful, detailed picture of her baby in heaven. I took the part of the baby and said, "Look Mommy, I'm up here with Jesus. I forgive you for what you did. I love you very much. Please do not grieve for me any more. And when you come to heaven I'll be here to meet you. I'll be swinging on the pearly gate, waiting for you."

A light broke over Sherry's face, and she asked for and received her baby's forgiveness. It was one of the most sacred moments I ever experienced. The room was filled with peace and we became aware of the quietness. The totally loving presence of God was there, and a cleansing light, like the warm touch of a sunbeam, covered us both.

The last area we dealt with was her need to forgive the young man who had gotten her pregnant and had insisted that she have an abortion. She had seven long years of scorching bitterness stored up against him. When she forgave him, the final chains that had held her captive for so long fell off. She felt a tender seed of God's love springing up in her heart. From that seed came a new life. She had been cleansed and healed from sin and guilt. She was left with a singing deep within her heart.

LIFE BEGINS

A baby is one of the greatest gifts we will ever receive. Yet we, as a nation and as individuals, put to death one and a half million of these precious gifts of life every year. In our country over twenty-five million women have become prisoners of liberation through abortion. They often go through life gripped with nagging guilt and sorrow. This is not a self-imposed guilt, as the feminists claim. It is not even a cultural guilt. It is a universal guilt. When God created us in his image, he implanted within each one of us a sense of right and wrong. It is wrong to take another human life regardless of whether or not that life is in the womb. A woman never forgets her abortion. Mother Teresa said it all: "For the rest of their lives they will never forget, that as mothers, they had killed their own children."

Biologists, who spend their lives studying human life at various stages, agree that life begins when the sperm and egg are joined at the point of conception. *Human life is never absent in the development of a human being.* But it's right here, at this critical point, that we must accept this fact: We *do* believe in a woman's right to control her own body. This "pro-choice" right is a God-given right for all humankind. However, we simply cannot ignore the truth that the time to exercise that right is when she is faced with the option of participating in sexual intercourse or not. Once that choice is acted upon, she becomes responsible for the outcome. If a new life is conceived, the pro-choice stance is no longer valid. That's where she must become a pro-lifer—where she gives that new life the same opportunity she was given when she was conceived—to live. Yet this fact is ignored by our laws and much of the woman's movement.

All of a child's physical traits are present at the moment of conception. The nervous system is developed by twenty days, and within three weeks the heart is beating. Brain activity is recorded at forty-five days. At six to seven weeks, all the organs are present. In eight weeks, a child can grasp an object; and at ten weeks, can suck its fingers and toes. At eleven weeks, when many women make the decision to abort, the baby is sensitive to pain.[1] When President Reagan made a speech in which he referred to the pain an unborn baby feels, he was literally mobbed by an angry, hostile press. Hugh Sidey referred to it with dripping sarcasm: [Reagan] "marched holier than thou into the forbidding swamps of abortion and teenage sex" (*TIME* magazine, March 21, 1983, p. 18). It is difficult to refute the evidence portrayed in the movie *The Silent Scream,* produced by Dr. Nathanson, which showed an actual abortion of an eleven-week-old baby. Nathanson demonstrated that long before the instrument had touched the baby, it was aware that an invasion had entered its sanctuary. When the suction tip hit the amniotic sac (the membrane surrounding the child), the baby jumped. He said as far as we know, the amniotic sac has no nerve fibers, so the child clearly does not feel, but senses something aggressive is happening and jumps away.

In the film, the infant's mouth opens in a silent scream, and the agitation that takes place as the abortion progresses is visible. The heart speeds up, the limbs move faster, the child turns more rapidly, and increased breathing takes place as the baby seeks to preserve its life. In the end, it loses the battle. Following the abortion another life, still warm from its mother's womb, is dropped into a waiting bucket and discarded at the end of the day. If children are not safe in their mothers' wombs, where are they safe?

The Supreme Court has decreed that abortion should be performed before the third month, and certainly not after the sixth month. In doing this, it has decided when life begins! "What is there at that point of the continuum that suddenly makes the fetus a living human?"[2] "Human life is on a continuum and is present the entire length of the continuum."[3]

Abortion

The Supreme Court created a law on the basis of one woman and one doctor. Because of this law, over twenty-five million babies have now been wiped out (Rowe vs. Wade, Nov. 22, 1973). By the end of the twentieth century, we will have killed forty-five million of our own children. This amounts to over 4,800 babies a day having their lives snuffed out. Within the first ten years of our country's period of legal abortion, "more than 15 million unborn children have had their lives snuffed out by legalized abortions. That is over *ten times* the number of Americans lost in ALL this nation's wars."[4]

As a nation, and as individuals, we have lost our reverence for God. The natural outcome of this is always the total loss of reverence for humanity and for one another.

My little five-year-old grandson, Shane, came over for lunch today. When I opened the door, there he stood on my front porch with his new Snoopy coloring book and crayons. After having his favorite food for lunch we sprawled out on the living room floor to color. It was there that Shane looked up at me with his big brown eyes and said, "Grandma, do you know what I'm going to be when I grow up? I'm going to be a minister." I looked at his dear little innocent face, and my eyes filled with tears. His father, grandfather and uncle are all ministers. It just may be that one day, Shane will also be a minister. But because I was in the middle of writing this chapter on abortion, my heart was torn and tender. I couldn't help but wonder how many other little children, who didn't get a chance to live, wanted to be a minister, an artist, or a scientist. How can taking a human life ever be right?

THEY'RE GONE

Jimmy would have been a farmer, Jeremy a priest.
Dennis would have joined the Army, Daniel the police.
Darcy would have gone to college, Jennifer to France.
Laura would have run for Congress if she'd only had the chance.
Larry would have played for Dallas, Christopher for fun.

Carlos would have raised a daughter, Anthony three sons.
Cindy would have been a writer, Jane an engineer.
Bonnie would have been your friend if only she were here.

Jason would have built cathedrals, Jonathon old cars.
Steven would have flown to China, Kevin to the stars.
Wendy would have made the clothes that Sharon would have
worn.
Carol would have changed the world if only she'd been born.

Chorus:

But they're gone, yes they're gone, now the time has come to
mourn
For millions of our children—gone before they're born.
We'll never know their faces, or who they might have been
But they're safe with their Creator—never (to) pass this way
again.[5]

THE INEVITABLE OUTCOME

How tragic that the safest place in all the world, the
mother's womb, has now become a chamber of death. Kill-
ing our unborn children is now a multi-billion dollar-a-year
industry in our country. In many cases abortion has simply
become an easy form of birth control. Seventy-six percent of
women today choose to have an abortion of convenience because having a baby "would change their life [job, school]."
Those who choose abortion because of rape or incest stand
at one percent.[6] (This is certainly opposite from the information pro-abortionists would have us believe.)

"Why do so many liberal and radical activists cham-
pion for nuclear disarmament to protect the sanctity of human life and then defend the destruction of one-and-a-half
million unborn babies each year? Are "sexual freedom" and
affluent life-styles finally more important than helpless, in-
convenient babies?"[7]

When one highly developed human being can decide
that a less-developed human should be terminated, and this
can be done legally and for profit, then we as individuals
and as a society have become less than human. "The cul-

tural environment for a human holocaust is present whenever any society can be misled into defining individuals as less than human and therefore devoid of value and respect."[8]

Since the policy of one child per family was established in China, having more than one child produces heavy financial penalties and fines. Parents can be dismissed from their jobs. They lose all of their educational and medical benefits, plus farmland and housing.

As a result, fifty-three million abortions were performed in China between 1979 and 1984. In 1983 alone, 14.4 million babies were aborted. Many of these abortions were done when the mother was six to nine months along.[9] "It's appalling . . . they're subjecting women to severe emotional and physical trauma. And they're encouraging, as well as committing widespread infanticide."[10]

Since couples can only have one child, many kill their baby girls at birth. A bucket is often placed in front of the delivery bed and if the newborn is a girl, she is immediately drowned. Parents want sons to carry on the family name and to care for them later in life. As a result, according to Chinese newspapers, the ratio of boy to girl children is as high as 5 to 1. The *People's Daily* newspaper, 1983, stated: "At present, the phenomenon of butchering, drowning and leaving female infants to die is very serious."[11] When human life loses its meaning, we become less significant than a litter of kittens.

In our own country, losing 1.5 million children a year is having a devastating result on us economically, culturally, and ethnically. Demographer Charles Westoff of Princeton, has estimated that 50 percent of young American women will bear either no children or only one child. In 1950, the population of the free Western world was 22 percent of the global population. In 1986, it was down to 15 percent. By the year 2030, it will be 9 percent. By the end of the twenty-first century, experts predict that it will be less than 5 percent. We must ask ourselves how much influence we will have in the world when our population continues to diminish at this rate? With one abortion taking place every twenty seconds, our population growth now is at zero.

THE HUMAN ISSUE

Today, loving couples longing for a baby must remain childless. Over two million couples in the United States are trying to become parents but can't. There are so few babies for adoption that couples must often wait up to ten years for a baby. Studies show that there are 1.5 million abortions in our country every year, and at the same time, there are 1.6 million *formal* requests for adoption. For every 100 couples seeking to adopt, only one child is available.

A woman who chooses not to abort, but to carry her baby full term and place it up for adoption in a loving home, finds that all medical and legal costs are paid. When she chooses not to abort, she can be spared from one of the most profound mistakes of her entire life. When she has an abortion she faces life-long consequences, physically, emotionally, psychologically, and spiritually. My friend was told, "No problem. You'll come in during the morning and go home a few hours later. It will all be over." But it is never "all over." I have been speaking around the country for years and have never talked to any woman from 15 to 50, who had an abortion and who did not cry when telling me about it. Even though years have past, the searing flame of guilt continues to burn—the sorrow remains, and sorrow doesn't stop with the woman. It is passed on to the doctors and nurses involved in performing abortions.

New information indicates that more and more of those in the medical profession are relunctant to do abortions. They find them "emotionally difficult and unpleasant." They acknowledge that they "feel a great sense of conflict about abortion." They have been trained to bring children into the world in a healthy state and that "doing an abortion is a real contradiction."[12]

Abortion is more than a feminist issue; it is a human issue that affects every one of us. The abortion issue will never be totally resolved by law. Legislation and education must join hands together if we are going to reach a solution. But the problem really goes much deeper. It is a basic problem of sin, a lack of our nation's character and of the citizens who dwell here. The respect for life is the one ingredient that holds us together as human beings—without that we are less than human. Today, that respect is absent, and we are in grave danger of losing our humanness. "The real question today is not, when does life begin, but what is the value of human life? We cannot diminish the value of one category of human life—the unborn—without diminishing the value of all human life."[13]

Elizabeth Goudge said, "Civilization is another word for respect of life." The whole question of abortion can be boiled down to the assumption that an unborn baby is something less than a human life. As a nation, we have lost our moral and spiritual direction by legalizing abortion. We have lost our God and we have lost our way.

We forget that all life comes from God and is very precious in His sight. It is God who places such dignity and value on each human life. We forget God's laws and standards do not change according to society's whims and desires. Abortion is wrong; it's always been wrong, and will be wrong in the future. Our decisions are never made in a vacuum. What we decide about abortion today affects our world for generations. It affects you. It affects me. It affects everyone around us. The law of cause and effect is permanently established in all of creation. God does not spare us from reaping the consequences of our choices. He is a God of infinite, unconditional love, but He is also a God of total justice who always acts consistently within His holy character. The Bible proclaims that life is precious, with each of us created in the image of God. We must seriously consider this overwhelming yet sobering fact.

In the end, who has the right to say, "It would not be good for this child to be born"?

Thought Question

CHAPTER TEN

1. Share one or two of your underlined thoughts.

2. List the three areas of forgiveness Sherry needed to deal with before complete healing could take place. Why was each area so important?

3. When does life first appear in the development of a human being? Where does life come from? Should this make a difference in our attitude toward abortion? If so, why?

4. What are some of the dangers we, as a people, face when human life loses its meaning?

5. What are some creative alternatives to abortion?

6. What would you say to a friend who was considering an abortion? How would you help her through her decision, regardless of her choice?

7. In the end, who has the right to say, "It would not be good for this child to be born"?

ELEVEN

The Sexual Revolution vs. God's Absolutes

If there is no God, all things are permissible.

TODAY THE BEAUTIFUL country of America is drowning in a sea of illicit sex. As a nation every form of sexuality is thrust upon us and our children through advertisements, television, movies, magazines, and books. There was time when the laws of nature, and the laws of God, were clearly known and understood in this country. We knew that a monogamous marital relationship was expected of us. We understood something of the moral and spiritual values of premarital chastity. Back in 1967, over 85 percent of all Americans still disapproved of premarital sex. Today, less than 15 percent think it is wrong, and we are reaping the disastrous outcome of that statistic. Marriage and sex have become totally separated in the liberated sexual revolution of the '80s.

> We have separated sex not only from love, but from attachment and commitment. The sexual liberation of the last 20

131

years has exposed the emptiness and unfulfilling nature of sex unattached to love. It is now easier for many young people to go to bed with each other than to form trusting or intimate relationships. It is easier for them to expose their bodies to a stranger than to expose their feelings; it has become less frightening.[1]

A guest on a recent talk show expressed the sentiments of our liberated society when he said, "Sex is simply a recreation as far as I'm concerned. I see no differences between it, or bowling, or baseball." That statement reflects how grossly infantile much of our society has become, and how close we are to moral and spiritual collapse. A recent survey showed 75 percent of our country's young men expect to have sex by the third date, and 80 percent by the fifth date. Sex has replaced baseball as the national pastime!

Perhaps nothing has ruined the lives, careers, and reputations of people more than the recent sexual revolution. It has produced divorce, abortion, incest, pornography, and the active homosexual lifestyle—resulting in a catastrophic increase of children being born into single-parent families, and leaving a trail of hurting, broken relationships. The suffering and horror from the numerous sexual diseases must also be added. As a result of our sexual revolution over twelve million cases of sexually transmitted diseases occur each year. This amounts to 38,000 new cases a day. Many of these are incurable. Almost daily, our newspapers tell us about the deadly disease of AIDS. Leading health authorities call it the "worst health problem of the century." The number of people dying daily from this disease is equivalent to the number of deaths of one jumbo 747 jet crashing every day. It is estimated that over three million people are infected with AIDS and do not know it. They can unknowingly transmit this disease to others for as long as ten years. Innocent partners are being infected. No one is safe!

Hundreds of thousands of little children have lost their innocence because of our sexual revolution. They are silently dying, mentally and psychologically, because they have been sexually abused and used by parents, teachers, relatives, and friends. They have become prisoners of liberation in their own homes and schools.

In our sexual revolution we have forgotten or ignored the truth that sex without love and commitment equals loneliness. It is often empty and degrading. In addition we have lost the innocence we had when we more clearly understood that sex was a beautiful gift from God and that he ordained our sexual instincts to be completed in marriage. We have lost the sense of wonder and beauty found in our God-given ability to express our sexuality in the sanctity of marriage—as the means of constantly renewing our love for and devotion to one another. But perhaps most tragically, we have lost our honor. Remember the scene from *Gone With the Wind* when Scarlett was pleading with Ashley to leave his wife and baby and run away with her? At one point she cried, "Oh, Ashley! Don't you see? There's *nothing* to keep us here!" To which Ashley replied, "Nothing? . . . Nothing except our honor."

What has become of our honor as persons and as a nation? Something inside us dies when we lose our honor, when we give in to the standards that go against everything we know within our hearts to be right. Our consciences have been deadened through our sexual revolution, and our moral values have been seared into numbness. Our spiritual landmarks are missing and we no longer have any moorings to cling to. We are held captive in a dark prison of liberation.

HOMOSEXUALITY

In this section on homosexuality, I use the term homosexual to mean the practicing or active homosexual. During thirty-eight years of ministry, my husband and I have known homosexuals who have chosen to live celibate lives in the same way unmarried heterosexuals choose to live celibate lives.

At the time of the Fall (Gen. 3:6), *all* of creation fell. Nature and the human race fell. We became separated from

God, and our fellowship with one another was marred. Even sexual relationships were affected by the Fall. Instead of man and woman becoming one, as ordained by God, we now have adultery, practicing homosexual and lesbian relationships, prostitution, incest, rape, and beastiality. All of these are distortions of the wholeness and oneness that God originally intended. They go against the purpose of God's plan for marriage and family life. Homosexuality is a perversion of the law of nature and violates the law of God. It is a distortion of the beauty of God's pattern for man and woman. Karl Barth stated that homosexuality is a "distortion of God's norm for His creation."

God created humans as two distinct creations, male *and* female. From Genesis to Revelation, sexuality is always in this context. The practicing homosexual lifestyle is not an alternative lifestyle, it is a departure from God's plan. God did not create man to use one another in this unnatural way. Thomas Aquinas called it the "sin against nature and an injury against our Creator." God intended sexual intercourse to take place between man and woman. It is obvious that the male and female bodies were designed in this way. The Bible condemns every form of sexual expression outside of heterosexual marriage.

WHAT HOMOSEXUALS WANT FROM SOCIETY

Many homosexuals want heterosexuals to change their beliefs concerning sexuality and morality. They want us to sanction their lifestyle and legitimize their immoral practices. They want us to believe that "being born gay, is just like being born left handed, or with red hair. It's a normal variation in the human species."[2] Yet, after years of studies, authorities tell us that the homosexual lifestyle is *learned*. "Homosexuality, the choice of a partner of the same sex for orgastic satisfaction, is not innate. There is no connection between sexual instinct and the choice of sexual object. Such an object choice is learned, acquired behavior."[3] Even the more liberal studies reveal that "Social scientists tell us that about 5% of all males and about half that percentage of all females have a confirmed sexual drive toward persons of their own sex."[4]

The problem is that practicing homosexuals want society to approve of their lifestyle. As a result, they have become a highly organized group whose one goal is nation-wide acceptance. They lobby in Congress for homosexuality to be taught to grade-school children as a normal, healthy, alternative form of sexual expression. There is an active group of homosexuals lobbying for the ordination of minis-ters and priests within nearly every denominational church structure.

While lobbying nationwide for acceptance, many homo-sexuals present their lifestyle in a totally distasteful way. Some of their parades become nothing more than a blatant display of debauchery. They are asking the impossible when they ask us to accept their immoral behavior as right and good.

The sexual union between two men, or two women, can never be genuine. It goes against the total being, physically, emotionally, and spiritually. It is a distorted substitute that ultimately brings tragedy, loneliness, and emptiness to those who choose this way of life. The Bible strictly forbids sodomy. It is a debilitating sexual practice. That is why our nation has laws forbidding it. (For a more detailed study of sodomy, read any scientific medical journal on the subject at your local library.) "From a purely biological perspective, sodomy, even apart from the trans-mission of AIDS, is an intrinsically unsanitary act."[5] Doctors and scientists warn that even monogamous sodomy is not a safe alternative. The fact is that less than one percent of practicing homosexuals have a monogamous relationship.

A study of the rise and fall of ancient history shows that the extent of homosexual practice affects the general corruption of a society. Richard Lovelace says, "Homosexual expression endangers the formation of sexual identity in boys and girls, the integrity of the family, and therefore the stability of the whole society."[6] He goes on to say that a degenerative process is set in motion when a people, a society, and a nation endorses the practice of homosexuality.

A SOLUTION

The Bible speaks very plainly against homosexuality. wherever the subject comes up. When dealing with the homosexual issue, we cannot ignore the fact that whatever rights we have as human beings have been given to us by God, and we are therefore subject to him. "The issue before us, at the bottom line, is not Gay Rights, but God's rights. We are to seek His will and not our own."[7]

God's call to each of us is to live a lifestyle in heterosexual marriage or single chastity. Today, many homosexuals are turning from their promiscuous lifestyle to one of celibacy, just as more and more single heterosexuals are choosing the celibate life out of obedience to God. God calls all of us to forsake our sinful ways, whatever they may be. In our sex-saturated society, this requires enormous discipline. God calls us to have compassionate concern for one another. Homosexuals need to renounce their active homosexual lifestyle, just as those who are not homosexuals need to renounce the homophobia that keeps us separated from one another.

God issues a loving, clear call for repentance. Each of us needs to be restored and renewed in our personal walk with Him. Homosexual activity can be altered and controlled through the forgiving, healing love of Jesus Christ, and the indwelling power of the Holy Spirit. Constructive therapy is available for all who want it. (See note 13 for a list of helpful resources.)

THE UNIVERSAL PLAGUE OF SIN

Whatever happened to sin?
Doesn't anyone sin anymore?
Does anyone believe in sin?

136

Is there no longer any personal responsibility for sin?
Is anyone guilty of sin?
What is sin?

We rarely hear the word sin mentioned in our twentieth century liberated society. People don't talk about it, ministers don't preach about it, and society doesn't believe in it. No one seems to take it seriously anymore and it has apparently slipped, unnoticed, from our vocabulary. "Does that mean that no sin is involved in all our troubles—sin with an 'I' in the middle? Is no one any longer guilty of anything? Guilty perhaps of a sin that could be repented and repaired or atoned for?"[8]

What is sin? Today we are more likely to call sin a mistake, a wrong doing, a crime, or unacceptable behavior. Yet, basically, sin is not something we do. Rather, sin is something that we are. What I am (a sinner) makes me do what I do. This is a law of life. The Bible tells us, "All have sinned and fall short of the glory of God" (Rom. 3:23). Webster defines sin as "a transgression of the law of God; disobedience of the divine will; moral failure."

What is sin?
Sin separates us from God.
Sin is satisfying a legitimate desire in an illegitimate way.
Sin suppresses the truth.
Sin creates a vacuum.
Sin never satisfies.
Sin is never enough.
Sin is selfishness.
Sin is destructive.
Sin gets worse. It never gets better.
Sin separates us from one another.

"The worst thing about sin is that its punishment could not be borne by the sinner alone. Why did one not realize that before it was too late?"[9]

When we reach the place in life when we honestly acknowledge that we are sinners desperately in need of a Savior then there is hope for our lives and our world. Only then can we begin to positively deal with the problems sin produces. G. K. Chesterton said, "The glad good news brought by the Gospel was the news of original sin." The fact that we are all sinners is the one certainty in life that can be universally validated. With this comes the single, critical truth that can turn us to our Lord and Savior, Jesus Christ. He has provided the only existing remedy for sin through His death on the cross. Scripture tells us, "For the wages of sin is death, but the gift of God is eternal life in Christ Jesus our Lord" (Rom. 6:23).

MORAL ABSOLUTES

A number of years ago my husband went to Germany to exchange thoughts with some German church leaders. One was an old German pastor who had gone through the Holocaust. This gentleman had been a friend of Dietrich Bonhoeffer, the German martyr who wrote *The Cost of Discipleship*. Both had witnessed the heartbreaking horror of Hitler as he forged across Europe leaving a trail of death, terror, and destruction.

One evening, in a voice brushed with sorrow, the pastor shared with my husband, "In the end, Hitler became god; he became the ultimate authority on the value of human life. When this happens, man becomes expendable." A long pause followed. Only the heavy sighs of anguished memories could be heard. Then this grand old man of God doubled up his fist and, in a clear voice, pounded the table and shouted, *"Man is not man—unless God is God!"* These words vibrated through the room and were locked forever in my husband's heart. He will never forget them nor the absolute truth of their meaning.

When the basis of all morality is removed, God is taken from our lives. When we lose God, we lose man. That is why Stalin could kill over twenty million of his own people; Hitler could send six million Jewish mothers, fathers, and little children to the gas chambers; Mao could murder sixty-five million people in his "Cultural Revolution," and Pol Pot could do away with three million Cambodians. These men had set themselves up as gods. They became, for a time, the final authority. As a result, man was indeed no longer man. Dostoyevski rightly summed it up when he said, "If there is no God, all things are permissible." That is where we find ourselves at the conclusion of the twentieth century.

No longer are there any moral absolutes that govern our relationships with one another. We are no longer accountable to anyone, and certainly not to God. We have become a nation of irresponsible people. Drug addicts blame their condition on drug dealers; alcoholics say their problem is a disease; pornographers say they are just meeting the demands of the people; homosexuals say it is the fault of their genes; rapists say they got the urge from movies; and abortions happen because everyone does it. All of our problems are due to someone else or something else. If we can't think of anyone else to blame, we can always say, "the devil made me do it."

We have become a nation of blameless, guiltless people who have confused liberation with democracy so that we can no longer discern freedom from responsibility, or good from evil. Aleksander Solzhenitsyn stated it well when he said: "When Western society was established, it was based on the idea that each individual limited his own behavior. Everyone understood what he could do and what he could not do. The law itself did not restrain people. Since then, the only thing we have been developing is rights, rights, rights, at the expense of duty."[10]

True democracy has always been founded on absolutes and moral and spiritual order. There isn't any area of life that has escaped the liberated permissiveness that has pervaded our nation during the past twenty years. Martin Marty (of the University of Chicago) calls it a "widespread sense of moral disarray." We have forgotten that it is our moral absolutes that set us apart as a civilized people.

GOD'S ABSOLUTES

One day, shortly before I began writing this book, my husband came home with a big smile on his face. He said, "Go into the library and you will find a surprise!" Well, I love surprises, so I went quickly. There on the desk sat a "Video-Writer Computer." I was overjoyed but apprehensive. I was afraid I could never learn how to use it. What if I pressed the wrong button and the whole manuscript disappeared! (It won't.) The next day, I got my instruction manual out and carefully followed each step. I leaned how to use my computer and now wonder how I ever wrote a book without it. However, I would have been totally lost without the instructions. Everything I need to know about my computer is written down in order to help and aid me in properly using it.

God left us a book of instructions to tell us all we need to know for living in the beautiful world He created. In the Bible, He gave ten simple steps called the Ten Commandments to follow.

THE TEN COMMANDMENTS (EXODUS 20:1–17)

1) You shall have no other gods before me (v. 3).
2) You shall not make for yourself an idol (v. 4).
3) You shall not misuse the name of the Lord your God (v. 7).
4) Remember the Sabbath day by keeping it holy (v. 8).
5) Honor your father and your mother (v. 12).
6) You shall not murder (v. 13).
7) You shall not commit adultery (v. 14).
8) You shall not steal (v. 15).
9) You shall not give false testimony against your neighbor (v. 16).
10) You shall not covet (v. 17).

The Ten Commandments were given to show us what God is like. They serve as a restraint in our lives to keep us close to God and to each other. They are the standards that keep us from becoming totally depraved. They are a light to show us the sin and weaknesses in our lives. They were not given to spoil our good times, but rather to protect us and keep us from ruining ourselves. They are ten different signposts directing us along life's pathway. The Ten Commandments are fixed absolutes. They are above culture. They do not change with the whims of each new generation. They are the same yesterday, today, and forever. They will remain unchanged thousands of years from now.

> These are not trifles of men but the commandments of the most high God, who watches over them with real earnestness, who vents his wrath upon those who despise them . . . . Therefore, it is not without reason that the Old Testament commands us to write the Ten Commandments on every wall and corner, and even on their garments . . . . We are to keep them incessantly before our eyes and constantly in our memory, and practice them in all our works and ways. [11]

When the Supreme Court removed the Ten Commandments from Kentucky schoolrooms (November 17, 1980), an enormous vacancy was left. We had no other moral code to offer our children.

Ted Koppel, of ABC *Nightline*, had this to say about the Ten Commandments:

> We have actually convinced ourselves that slogans will save us. Shoot up if you must, but use a clean needle. Enjoy sex whenever and with whomever you wish, but wear a condom. No! The answer is no. Not because is isn't cool or smart or because you might end up in jail or dying in an AIDS ward, but no because it's wrong, because we have spent 5,000 years as a race of rational human beings, trying to drag ourselves out of the primeval slime by searching for truth and moral absolutes. In its purest form, truth is not a polite tap on the shoulder. It is a howling reproach. What Moses brought down from Mount Sinai were not the Ten Suggestions. [12]

When Jesus was here on earth, He summed up the Ten Commandments in a way every person on earth could understand. He said we are to "Love the Lord your God with all your heart and with all your soul and with all your mind. . . . Love your neighbor as yourself" (Matt. 22:37, 39).

Certainly we can live by two simple rules, can't we? To love God. To love one another. Why have we made God's absolutes so complicated?

UNCHANGING TRUTH

Truth is truth whether we believe it or not. Our unbelief never alters the truth. Truth is fixed. Two plus two will always equal four. The law of gravity is a fixed law of the universe. If we say, "I don't believe in the law of gravity," that does not change the law. When an apple drops from a tree, it still falls to the ground, regardless of what we want to believe. There is no way we could live in a world devoid of truth—where there are no absolutes.

Truth can never be whatever we choose to make it. Our country was founded on objective truth. The Constitution, based on objective truth, upholds that truth and rules over humankind. The principle behind objective truth is always the fact that there is a God who is there. Subjective truth, on the other hand, says that whatever I, as an individual, think is true becomes truth. No nation can survive on subjective truth where wrong could become right tomorrow and where each person does what is right in his or her own eyes.

In our permissive, liberated culture, we have lost God's unchanging truth, and in the process, we have lost God. When we lose God, we lose the very cornerstone of truth. When we no longer have a basis for determining right from wrong, good from evil, we will, in the words of Aleksandr Solzhenitsyn, "decline to the status of animals." Today our moral distinctions are dissolving into a sea of indulgence. There is no longer any good or evil, no unchanging truth, no solid foundation upon which to build a life.

It's all shifting sand. Whatever pleases me has become truth.

As a nation and as indiviudals we have become followers of culture instead of followers of God. Humankind would have destroyed itself long ago without our God-given built-in value system. When we become totally liberated from our moral and spiritual values, we stand on the brink of moral disintegration. Each day our global village tilts a little closer toward total self-annihilation. We forget that everything is not okay. There are rules in life. There is truth. There are absolutes. Some things are wrong regardless of what we think, and some things are wrong, even if two consenting adults say it isn't wrong. We want to be the ones who decide what is right and wrong. We want to relegate *who* God is and *how* He should act. But God can never be relegated. He is the Alpha and the Omega, the beginning and the end. He is the center of the universe, not us. God's existence is not dependent upon whether we believe in Him or not. God is. Period. And without God, there is no humanity. "Man is not man, unless God is God."

God has implanted His law within each one of His beloved creations. He said, "I will put my law in their minds and write it on their hearts. I will be their God, and they will be my people" (Jer. 31:33). Our moral and spiritual values are rooted in the Bible. It alone gives us the ultimate standard of right and wrong. It alone tells us how to live. It teaches us the eternal values of love, faith, loyalty, respect, trust, truthfulness, faithfulness, chastity, fidelity, and honor. We, as a nation and as individuals, must return to the moral and spiritual unchanging truths of God's Word.

God asks for nothing more from each of us than our life. And He asks for nothing less.

Thought Questions

CHAPTER ELEVEN

1. Share one or two of your underlined thoughts.

2. What dangers do you see as a result of our sexual revolution? What have we lost because of it?

3. Why do you think the Bible condemns all forms of sexual expression outside of the heterosexual marriage?

4. How would you help your child to understand the homosexual issue?

5. What is your definition of sin?

6. Why do you think God gave us the Ten Commandments?

7. How does Matthew 22:37–39 sum up the Ten Commandments?

8. What is the difference between objective truth and subjective truth?

9. Why is it so important to us and to our world that God's truth never changes?

10. What unchanging truths do you want to pass on to your children?

TWELVE

The Great Liberator

The closer we get to God, the more we become our true self.

THERE IS an unforgettable scene at the end of the movie, *The Mission*. After all the tribes are ruthlessly murdered in the name of politics and religion, the general who ordered the massacre, turns to the bishop, and with a guilt-releasing shrug of his shoulders says,

Well—thus is the world.

In a rare moment of truth, the bishop responded,

No, señor, thus we have made the world.

What kind of a world have we made for ourselves and future generations? Are we content with what has transpired during the past twenty years in our society, and in our relationships with one another? Or has the price we paid for our so-called liberation been too steep? Where is the success, happiness, and peace of mind we were promised? Have we been lured into the flower-tossed sea of unrestrained freedom, only to discover, too late, the danger of being sucked into a hopeless undertow of despair?

As we prepare to enter the twenty-first century, we can no longer ignore the dilemma facing us. Are we content to live in a nation that is fast becoming morally and spiritually bankrupt? How are we going to solve the dichotomy of intensely longing to belong to someone while at the same time insisting on total liberation? Is it too late to change the direction we are headed?

Robert Schuller said, "If you want to change your world, change yourself." One way we can change as individuals is by looking at what our liberation without responsibility has produced. We may have to be honest enough to admit we don't like much of what we see. If we reach that conclusion, then we can begin to examine the weaknesses of this ideology. Only when the weaknesses are recognized and dealt with, can they become strengths. "We can learn nothing in this world until we have learned our own weaknesses."[1] In this book we looked at some of our weaknesses. If we have learned something about them, there is hope. Then we can constructively reevaluate all that we have been through the past twenty years. New value systems can emerge out of the chaos of broken relationships and shattered dreams. We can rebuild the bridges of life that have rotted out through our neglect and unconcern. "Destruction and construction always go hand in hand."[2] The days of destructive "liberation" are over. We must ask what *we* can do to restore our moral and spiritual values.

Elias Chacour, in his excellent book, *The Blood Brothers* quotes one of his professors saying:

> If there is a problem somewhere . . . this is what happens. Three people will try to do something concrete to settle the issue. Ten people will give a lecture analyzing what the three are doing. One hundred people will comment or condemn the ten for their lecture. One thousand people will argue about the problem. And ONE PERSON—only one— will involve himself deeply in the true solution . . . "Now," he asked gently, his penetrating eyes meeting each of ours in turn, "which person are you?"[3]

This is the question all of us must answer; which person are we at this time in our history?

I believe we are standing on the threshold of a new beginning in our country. The days where the traditional family was scorned are disappearing. Latest statistics show marriage is now "in," and divorce is "out." Eighty-eight percent of all Americans want to see a return to traditional family ties. The time has come for each of us to stop letting the 12 percent speak for the 88 percent. Most Americans are still tenaciously committed to marriage and the family. Having babies in the conventional way, with one mother and one father, is on the rise. Most of us want mature, caring, lasting relationships. Let's join the 90 percent of our nation who are reacting negatively to the sexual revolution and together bring about a real change. Let's bring back the values that made our nation great—values like commitment, integrity, honesty, trust, and fidelity. Let's give children some meaningful "shoulds" and "should nots" to guide them along life's pathway. Let's return to our churches and our faith in God. Let's not pass up this golden opportunity to change our world.

Mother Teresa had one goal in life and that was, "to do something beautiful for God." What a difference it would make if each of us would daily choose to do something beautiful for God and for one another.

A NEW BEGINNING

Today is a lovely spring day drenched in beauty. Warm beams of sunlight dance across the jewel-like blossoms of the rhododendrons and azaleas; and flowering apple trees take on the soft color of dreams. Mount Rainier, dressed in all of its snow-covered majesty, is etched against a brilliant blue sky, and the joyous songs of the birds mingle with the delicate fragrance of lilacs. The beauty of it all caught my heart when I took my morning walk. I felt as though I was given a tiny peak into heaven. The earth was alive and rejuvenated. Everything was new, lovely, and clean after the cold dreariness of winter.

Spring is my favorite time of the year. It always reminds me of God's eternal plan for renewal. Just as nature needs to be constantly restored, so people must be daily renewed, physically, mentally, and spiritually, or we will become as dry and barren as the winter leaves. Few things in life compare to the loveliness of a new and fresh beginning, and that is exactly what God has promised us.

When God created us, He created us with an innate knowledge that there is someone greater than we are; someone of supreme importance and value; someone who dearly loves us and who has an eternal plan and purpose for our lives. And that someone is God. He created us with an unquenchable longing to know Him and worship Him. Saint Augustine said we were all created with a built-in vacuum that can only be filled by God. We were created to, "glorify God and enjoy Him forever." Everything we need to know about God can be known through the beauty of His creation and through His Word, the Bible. We were created to believe in Him. In fact, believing in God is completely normal. It is abnormal not to believe in Him.

Happiness is knowing God and understanding what we believe. But what are we to believe? C. S. Lewis, that great English scholar, said belief always starts with just two words; "God is." "In the beginning was the Word, and the Word was with God, and the Word was God . . . the Word became flesh and made his dwelling among us" (John 1:1, 14).

Two thousand years ago, God visited this planet Earth. "The Word became flesh and made his dwelling among us." The Word's name was Jesus. He walked our streets, ate our food, and showed us the meaning and purpose of life. He taught us the significance of peace, joy, and true love. He showed us how to live, and how to love. When He finished teaching us all our finite minds could understand, He went to the cross where He died to pay the penalty for our sin. That was something we could never do for ourselves. He rose again on the third day, conquering for all time and eternity two of our greatest enemies, sin and death.

Today, the cross of Jesus Christ stands high on churches throughout the world. It is a continual reminder to every passerby that Jesus provided the only remedy for sin on earth. Forgiveness is offered to all who receive Him as Lord and Savior.

The Judeo-Christian faith is the only religion in the world that deals with the problem of sin. It is also the only religion that says, "God so loved the world that He gave." That is the most profound statement ever made. Everything we need to know about God is wrapped up in it. From those words we learn that

God is a loving God.

God is a giving God.

All the great religious masterpieces of art, all the beautiful anthems ever played or sung, and all the books and poems ever written about God have tried to express this magnificent truth. Nowhere in any other world religion, is there a God who loved the world. Instead, you often find other beliefs based on fear and superstition, talking to dead spirits, or trying to somehow appease angry gods. Ancient Greeks dealt with horrible fearful gods, and the Roman gods were jealous and angry. It has never been said that there was a God who loved the world—except in the Bible. "For God so loved the world, that He gave His one and only Son, that whoever believes in Him shall not perish but have eternal life" (John 3:16). Jesus tells us we are born again (John 3:5–7), when we choose, by an act of our will, to take God at His word and receive Him as our Lord and Savior. We are born spiritually. We are given a new life and a new beginning.

There is a delightful story about a little boy who lived in Holland. He spent the long winter months building a boat to sail on the lake in the park the following year. At last spring arrived and his boat was finished. He painted it a shiny candy-apple red and trimmed it with white sails. It was a work of art to his wondering eyes. His mother packed him a lunch and off he went to the park. When he reached the lake, a feeling of radiant joy filled every part of his body. The day he had worked for so long had arrived!

As he stooped down to launch his boat, he made sure the string he had tied to it was secure. Oh, how pretty his red sailboat looked bouncing up and down on the sun-kissed water! However, it wasn't long before a great gust of wind came and tore the boat's string from the boy's hand. In absolute horror, he watched his little red boat sail out to the middle of the lake, around the bend, and out of sight. All day long the little boy ran up and down the shore searching for his boat. At nightfall, he realized it was gone and a great sorrow fell upon him. He went home broken-hearted.

The summer months passed, and though he continued to search for his boat, he never found it. One autumn day, the little boy went down to the village square. He looked in the window of one of the shops and there to his complete surprise was his red sailboat! He burst through the door, and joyfully asked the owner to return it to him. But the owner said the boat was his. He had bought it just yester-day. He said the boy could have it if he paid for it. The price was five dollars, an enormous amount of money for any lit-tle boy. And so the boy ran all the way home. He emptied out his entire bank and ran back to the store as fast as he could. He gave the owner the money and once again the boat belonged to him. As he left the shop, he hugged his little red sailboat tightly to his heart, and with a voice full of happy tears and laughter said, "Oh! Don't you see? You're twice mine! I made you and I bought you!"

That is exactly what God did for us. He made us in the first place. Then we rebelled against Him . . . went our own way and ignored Him. The Bible describes this as being "lost in sin." Yet Jesus came to seek and to save all who were lost. When He found us, He bought us back. And the price He paid was his very own life's blood. This is the costly reality of the Cross. This is the new life and the new beginning God promises to all who receive him.

Everything good in life starts with God. He alone is the Great Liberator. True freedom comes from knowing and loving God. Our true identity is in Him. In fact, the closer we get to God, the more we become our true self.

Jesus said, "Then you will know the truth, and the truth will set you free" (John 8:32). That is what this book is all about. Freedom—God's kind of liberated freedom.

True liberation is Jesus and you,
Together,
Always.

Thought Questions

CHAPTER TWELVE

1. Share one or two of your underlined thoughts.

2. Why is it so important to examine our own weaknesses as well as the weaknesses we find in today's culture?

3. Which value systems would you like to see restored?

4. What are you willing to do to bring the needed change in your life? In our country?

5. What positive, encouraging signs do you see taking place in our nation today?

6. In what way is God bringing renewal and restoration to your life today?

7. What two enemies did Jesus conquer on the cross? How does this make you feel?

8. Write out your definition of a Christian.

9. How would you describe the way God is working in your life today?

10. In what way has reading this book been helpful to you?

Notes

■ ▭▭▭▭▭ ■

CHAPTER ONE

[1]Charles Colson, *Loving God* (Grand Rapids: Zondervan, 1983), 17.

[2]Chaim Potak, *Davita's Harp* (New York: Knopf, 1985), 269.

[3]Wolf Bierman, East German poet, quoted in *Time* (January 1, 1990), 59.

CHAPTER TWO

[1]Al Greene, "A Witness to the Western World," *The Mind Field* 6, no. 3 (1987): 1.

[2]Information gathered from Dr. Harry MacDonald's Leadership Seminar, Seattle, Wash., 1987; see also: Will and Ariel Durant, *The Story of Civilization*, "The Age of Reason Begins" (New York: Simon & Schuster, 1961), 639.

[3]Pat Robertson, *America's Date With Destiny* (Nashville: Thomas Nelson, 1986), 44.

[4]Ibid., 47.

[5]Ibid., 48.

[6]Ibid., 21.

[7]Ibid., 194.

[8] "Declaration of Feminism", (November 1971), as quoted in material distributed by the LaHaye organization "Concerned Women of America."

[9]Allan Bloom, *The Closing of the American Mind* (New York: Simon and Schuster, 1987), 143.

[10] Kris Kristofferson, "Me and Bobbie McGee" copyright 1969; reported by Lance Morrow in *Time*, (January 11, 1988), 16.

[11]Bloom, *The Closing of the American Mind*, 228.

[12] Roger Rosenblatt, "The Freedom of the Damned," *Time* (October 6, 1986), 98.

CHAPTER THREE

[1]Mike Mason, *The Mystery of Marriage* (Portland, Ore.: Multnomah Press, 1985), 91.

[2]Mason, *The Mystery of Marriage*, 91.

[3]Richard Foster, *Money, Sex and Power* (San Francisco: Harper & Row, 1985), 93.

[4]Robert C. Roberts, "Reconcilable Differences," *Christianity Today* (June 12, 1987), 6.

[5]Mason, *The Mystery of Marriage*, 47.

[6]Ibid., 87.

[7]Ibid., 15.

[8]Alan Loy McGinnis, *The Romance Factor* (San Francisco: Harper & Row, 1982), 159.

[9]Elizabeth Goudge, *The Scent of Water* (London: Hodder and Stoughton, 1963), 108.

[10]Foster, *Money, Sex and Power*, 7.

CHAPTER FOUR

[1] "Women, Work and Babies; Can America Cope?" NBC *White Paper*, (March 16, 1985).

[2]Mary Jo Bane, *Tulsa World* (August 21, 1977); Associated Press (as quoted in material distributed by LaHaye organization "Concerned Women of America").

[3]Vivian Gornick, *The Daily Illini* (April 25, 1981), as quoted in material distributed by the LaHaye organization "Concerned Women of America."

[4]*Woman's Liberation*, Notes from the Second Year, as quoted in material distributed by the LaHaye organization "Concerned Women of America."

[5]Nehemiah 4:10.

[6]Bloom, *The Closing of the American Mind*, 57.

[7]Ibid.

[8]Daniel Patrick Moynihan, *Family and Nation* (New York: Harcourt Brace Jovanovich, 1986), 194.

[9]Lee Iacocca, *Iacocca, An Autobiography,* (New York: Bantam, 1984), 3.

[10]Ibid.

[11]Foster, *Money, Sex and Power*, 248.

[12]Karl Menninger, *Whatever Became of Sin?* (San Francisco: Harper and Row, 1985), 248.

[13]Mason, *The Mystery of Marriage*, 107.

CHAPTER FIVE

[1]Betty Friedan, *The Feminine Mystique* (New York: Dell, 1963), 296.

[2]Ibid., 294.

Notes

[3]Elizabeth Goudge, *The Eliots of Dameroshay* (London: Hodder and Stoughton, 1957), 39.

[4]Janet Burton, Linda Ditlmer, and Cheri Loveless, *What's A Smart Woman Like You Doing at Home?* (Washington, D.C.: Acropolis, 1986), 42.

[5]Friedan, *The Feminine Mystique*, 296.

[6]Lucy Scott and Meredith Joan Angwin, *Time Out for Motherhood* (Los Angeles: Jeremy P. Tarcher, 1986), 108. Distributed by St. Martins Press, New York; requests for permission: Jeremy P. Tarcher, Inc., 9110 Sunset Blvd., Los Angeles, CA 90069.

[7]Alvin P. Sanoff, "The Mixed Legacy of Women's Liberation," *U.S. News & World Report* (February 17, 1990), 61.

[8]Christine Davidson, *Staying Home Instead*, (Lexington, Mass.: D. C. Heath & Co., 1986), 10.

[9]"Women, Work, and Babies; Can America Cope?" *NBC White Paper* (March 6, 1985).

[10]United States Department of Labor.

[11]Claudia Wallis, "The Child Care Dilemma" *Time*, (June 22, 1987), 56.

[12]Ibid.

[13]Ibid.

[14]Burton White, Psychologist Center for Parent Education; Newton, Massachusetts.

[15]Arthur S. DeMoss, *The Rebirth of America* (Arthur S. DeMoss Foundation, 1986), 86.

[16]Peter Jennings, *ABC News Closeup* (transcript 19), 1987.

[17]Morton H. Shaevitz, "Why Men Confuse the Women They Love," *Reader's Digest* (November 1987), 65–66.

[18]Daly Carson, "The Feminist in the Family: the Femme Fatale?" *Fidelity* 2, no. 6 (May 1983), 13.

[19]Burton, *What's A Smart Woman Like You Doing at Home?* 18.

[20]Goudge, *The Eliots of Damerosehay*, 39.

CHAPTER SIX

[1]Mary Jo Bane, *Tulsa World* (August 21, 1977), Associated Press; as quoted in material distributed by the LaHaye organization "Concerned Women of America."

[2]Elizabeth Goudge, *Green Dolphin Country* (London: Hodder and Stoughton, 1944), 197.

[3]Dee Jepsen, *Women Beyond Equal Rights* (Waco, Tex.: Word, 1984), 157.

CHAPTER SEVEN

[1]Matthew 22:37–39.

[2]C. S. Lewis, *The Four Loves* (New York: Harcourt Brace Jovanovich, 1960), 10.

[3]Jepsen, *Women Beyond Equal Rights,* 217.

[4]Ibid., 89.

[5]Martin Luther, from his Fourth Thesis.

[6]Pierre Teilhard de Chardin.

CHAPTER EIGHT

[1]Genesis 3:12.

[2]Lynette and Thomas Long, *The Handbook for Latchkey Children and Their Parents,* (New York: Arbor House, 1983), 89.

[3]Moynihan, *Family and Nation,* 147.

[4]Ibid., 9.

[5]Ibid., 168.

[6]Peter Jennings, ABC, *News Closeup* (transcript 19).

[7]Ibid.

[8]Bloom, *The Closing of the American Mind,* 119.

[9]Richard Halverson, taken from "Perspective" (Nov. 9, 1977), Washington, D.C.

[10]Alan Loy McGinnis, *The Romance Factor* (San Francisco: Harper & Row, 1982), 138.

[11]Edith Schaeffer, *Forever Music* (Nashville: Thomas Nelson, 1986), 42.

CHAPTER NINE

[1]Jerry R. Kirk, *The Mind Polluters* (Nashville: Thomas Nelson, 1985), 31.

[2]Ibid., 32.

[3]Statistics supplied to the National Federation for Decency by Dr. Shirley O'Brien, University of Arizona.

[4]Kirk, *The Mind Polluters,* 27.

[5]Betty Wein, "Pornography on the March" *Readers Digest* (November 1987), 153; Excerpted with permission. Originally appeared in *World Media Report, Winter 1986,* "The Chilling Effect of Pornography" by Betty Wein.

Notes

[6]Kirk, *The Mind Polluters*, 27, 28.

[7]Ibid., 65.

[8]Ibid., 69.

[9]Allan Bloom, *The Closing of the American Mind*, 51.

[10]Kirk, *The Mind Polluters*, 30.

[11]Ibid., 29.

[12]The Meese Commission, 1986.

[13]Wein, "Pornography on the March," 158.

[14]For further study on pornography, see Dr. Jerry Kirk's *The Mind Polluters* (Nashville: Nelson, 1985).

Addresses for information on what you can do to help:

Morality in Media
475 Riverside Dr., Rm. 239–RD,
New York, NY 10115

The National Coalition Against Pornography
Dept RD
800 Compton Rd., Suite 9248
Cincinnati, OH 45231

Citizens for Decency through Law, Inc.
William Swindell, National Director
2331 W. Royal Palm Rd.
Phoenix, AZ 85021

National Christian Association
Brad Curl
P.O. Box 40945
Washington, D.C. 20016

CHAPTER TEN

[1]Francis Schaeffer, and C. Everett Koop, *Whatever Happened to the Human Race?* (Old Tappan, N. J.: Revell, 1979), 40.

[2]Bart Tarman, "Abortion: A Review with Critical Reflections on Our Church's Most Recent Documents," *Presbyterian Pro-Life*, (1984), 3.

[3]Ibid.

[4]Ronald Reagan, *Abortion and the Conscience of the Nation* (Nashville: Thomas Nelson, 1984), 15.

[5]Words and Music by Paul and Teri Reisser; Copyright 1985. All rights reserved. Used with Permission.

[6]"Family Planning Perspectives," July 1988, reported in *MS Magazine*, April 1989; as quoted in *Leadership* (Spring 1989), 81.

[7]Ron Sider, "Abortion Is Not the Only Issue," *Christianity Today* (July 14, 1989), 28.

[8]William Brennan, *Medical Holocaust* (Sioux City, S.D.: Norland, 1980).

[9]Walter Hatch, Ministry of Public Health, China, *Seattle Times*, (January 12, 1986), 1.

[10]Stephen Mosher, *Broken Earth; The Rural Chinese*, as reported by Walter Hatch in the *Seattle Times* (January 12, 1986), 1.

[11]*The People's Daily*, 1983, as reported by Walter Hatch in the *Seattle Times* (January 12, 1986), 1.

[12]From *The Sacramento Bee* (January 8,1990), 1.

[13]Reagan, *Abortion and the Conscience of the Nation*, 22.

[14]Ibid., 18.

CHAPTER ELEVEN

[1]Willard Gaylin, "Prime Time on the Couch," *TV Guide*, (October 4, 1986), 6.

[2]Alan Medinger, "A Life Determined Before Birth?" *Presbyterian Communique* (Mar/April, 1988): 10.

[3]Charles W. Socarides as quoted in Medinger, "A Life Determined Before Birth?"

[4]Foster, *Money, Sex and Power*, 110.

[5]Gene Antonio, *The AIDS Cover-up* (San Francisco: Ignatius, 1987), 110.

[6]Richard F. Lovelace, *Homosexuality; What Should Christians Do About It?* (Old Tappan, N.J.: Revell 1984), 105.

[7]Jerry R. Kirk, *The Homosexual Crisis* (Nashville: Nelson, 1986), 15.

[8]Menninger, *Whatever Became of Sin?* 15.

[9]Goudge, *Green Dolphin Country*, 127.

[10]Aleksandr Solzhenitsyn, quoted in *Time* (July 24, 1989), 60.

[11]Lovelace, *Homosexuality; What Should Christians Do About It?* 78.

[12]Ted Koppel, *ABC News Nightline*; at Duke University Commencement as quoted in *Time* (June 22, 1987), 69.

Notes

[13]Addresses for organizations to help homosexuals:

Courage
Rev. John Harvey O.S.F.S.
P.O. Box 913
Old Chelsea
New York, NY 10113

Exodus International
P.O. Box 2121
San Rafael, CA 94912

Love in Action
P.O. Box 2655
San Rafael, CA 94912

Outpost
P.O. Box 422
Minneapolis, MN 55414

Exodus International (Europe)
Box 3
Wirral Merseyville
England, L49 6NY

CHAPTER TWELVE

[1]Elizabeth Goudge, *Child From the Sea*, (London: Hodder and Stoughton, 1970), 589.

[2]Goudge, *Green Dolphin Country*, 281.

[3]Elias Chacour and David Hazard, *The Blood Brothers* (Grand Rapids: Zondervan, 1986), 129.

Bibliography

Bloom, Allan. *The Closing of the American Mind.* New York: Simon and Schuster, 1987.

Bridges, Jerry. *The Pursuit of Holiness.* Colorado Springs: NavPress, 1984.

Brownmiller, Susan. *Against Our Will.* New York: Simon & Schuster, 1975.

Burton, Linda, Janet Dittmer, and Cheri Loveless. *What's A Nice Woman Like You Doing At Home?* Washington D.C.: Acropolis Books, 1986.

Cardozo, Arlene Rossen. *Women At Home.* Garden City, N.Y.: Doubleday.

Cahill, Mary Ann. *The Heart Has Its Own Reasons.* Franklin Park, Illinois: LeLeche League International, 1983.

Chacour, Elias, and David Hazard, *The Blood Brothers.* Old Tappan, N.J.: Chosen Books, Revell, 1984.

Colson, Charles. *Loving God.* Grand Rapids: Zondervan, 1983.

Colson, Charles. *Kingdoms in Conflict.* Grand Rapids: Zondervan with William Morrow, 1987.

Davidson, Christine. *Staying Home Instead.* Lexington, Mass: D. C. Heath & Co., Lexington Books, 1986.

DeMoss, Arthur S. *The Rebirth of America.* Philidelphia: Arthur S. DeMoss Foundation, 1986. ???

Elliot, Elizabeth. *Love Has A Price Tag.* Ann Arbor, Mich.: Servant, 1979.

Foster, Richard. *Money, Sex and Power.* New York: Harper & Row, 1985.

Friedan, Betty. *The Feminine Mystique.* New York: Dell Publishing Co., 1963.

Garton, Jean. *Who Broke The Baby?* Minneapolis: Bethany House, 1979.

Gaylin, Willard, M.D. "Prime Time on the Couch." *TV Guide* (Oct. 4, 1986), 4.

Goudge, Elizabeth. *Green Dolphin Country.* London: Hodder and Stoughton, 1970.

——— *City of Bells.* London: Duckworth, 1936.

——— *Child From The Sea.* New York: Coward McCann, 1970.

——— *Towers In The Mist.* London: Hodder and Stoughton, 1938.

Hunter, Brenda. *Where Have All The Mothers Gone?* Grand Rapids: Zondervan, 1982.

Bibliography

Horton, Marilee. *Free To Stay At Home: A Woman's Alternative*. Waco, Tex.: Word, 1982.

Iacocca, Lee, with William Novak. *An Autobiography*. New York: Bantam Books, 1984.

Jepsen, Dee. *Women Beyond Equal Rights*. Waco, Tex.: Word, 1984.

Kirk, Dr. Jerry. *The Homosexual Crisis*. Nashville: Nelson, 1986.

————— *The Mind Polluters*. Nashville: Nelson, 1985.

Lewis, C. S. *The Four Loves*. New York: Harcourt, 1960.

Long, Lynette and Thomas. *The Handbook For Latchkey Children and Their Parents*. New York: Arbor House, 1983.

Lovelace, Richard F. *Homosexuality; What Should Christians Do About It?* Old Tappan, N.J.: Power Books, Revell, 1984.

Marshall, Peter, Jr., and David Manuel, Jr. *The Light and The Glory*. Old Tappan, N.J.: Revell, 1977.

Mason, Mike. *The Mystery of Marriage*. Portland, Ore.: Multnomah Press, 1985.

Menninger, Karl, M.D. *Whatever Became of Sin?* New York: Hawthorn Books, 1973.

McGinnis, Alan Loy. *The Romance Factor*. San Francisco: Harper & Row, 1982.

Merrill, Dean. "After School Orphans." *Christianity Today*, (August 10, 1984).

Moore, Dorothy and Raymond. *Home Grown Kids*. Waco, Tex.: Word, 1981.

Moynihan, Daniel Patrick. *Family and Nation*. New York: Harcourt Brace Jovanovich, 1986.

Nathanson, Bernard. *Aborting America*. Toronto: Cycle Books, 1979.

NBC News White Paper. "Women, Work, & Babies, Can America Cope?" (March 16, 1985), NBC Inc. Copyright, with Jane Pauley. Reported by: Lisa Myers, Jack Reynolds. Executive Producer, Robert Rogers.

O'Brien, Patricia. *Staying Together*. Random House, 1977.

Peterson, Eugene H. *A Long Obedience*. Downers Grove, Ill.: InterVarsity Press, 1980.

Robinson, Pat. *America's Date With Destiny*. Nashville: Nelson, 1986.

Schaeffer, Francis, and C. Everett Koop. *Whatever Happened to the Human Race?* Old Tappan, N.J.: Revell, 1979.

Schaeffer, Francis. *He Is There and He Is Not Silent*. Wheaton, Ill.: Tyndale House, 1972.

Schaeffer, Edith. *Forever Music*. Nashville: Nelson, 1986.

Scott, Lucy, and Meredith Joan Angwin. *Time Out For Motherhood*. New York: St. Martin's Press, 1986.

Smalley, Gary, and John Trent. *The Gift of Honor*. Nashville: Nelson, 1987.

Stafford, Tim. *Knowing the Face of God*. Grand Rapids: Zondervan, 1986.

Walton, Russ. *One Nation Under God*. Old Tappan, N.J.: Revell, 1975.

Wheat, Ed. *Love Life for Every Married Couple*. Grand Rapids: Zondervan, 1980.

Willke, John C., *Handbook on Abortion*. Cincinnati: Hays Publishing Co., 1971.

Welsh, Patrick. *Tales Out of School*. New York: Viking, 1986.

Zimmerman, Martha. *Should I Keep My Baby?* Grand Rapids: Zondervan.